# Current Issues in Ethiopian Private Higher Education Institutions: Opportunities and Challenges

Wossenu Yimam & Mulu Nega

FSS Research Report No. 9

**Forum for Social Studies (FSS)**
**Addis Ababa**

© 2012 by the authors and Forum for Social Studies (FSS)

All rights reserved.

Printed in Addis Ababa

Typesetting & Layouts: Konjit Belete

ISBN: 978- 99944-50-46-6

Forum for Social Studies (FSS)
P.O. Box 25864 code 1000
Addis Ababa, Ethiopia
Email: fss@ethionet.et
Web: www.fssethiopia.org.et

This Research Report was published with a core grant from the Civil Society Support Program (CSSP).

## Table of Contents

| | Page |
|---|---|
| **List of Abbreviations** | v |
| **List of Tables and Figure** | vi |
| **Acknowledgement** | vii |
| **Abstract** | viii |

| | | | Page |
|---|---|---|---|
| 1. | **INTRODUCTION** | | 1 |
| | 1.1 | Background of the study | 1 |
| | 1.2 | Statement of the problem | 3 |
| | 1.3 | Objectives of the study | 5 |
| | 1.4 | Scope of the study | 6 |
| 2. | **CONCEPTUAL AND THEORETICAL FRAMEWORK** | | 7 |
| | 2.1 | The forces that underlie privatization in higher education | 7 |
| | 2.2 | Conceptualizing privatisation of higher education | 9 |
| | 2.3 | The public-private partnership | 10 |
| | 2.4 | Factors affecting the behaviour and functioning of PHEIs | 14 |
| | 2.5 | The conceptual framework of the study | 22 |
| | 2.6 | The PHEIs context in Ethiopia | 23 |
| 3. | **METHODOLOGY OF THE STUDY** | | 25 |
| | 3.1 | Data sources | 25 |
| | 3.2 | Sampling techniques and procedures | 25 |
| | 3.3 | Data collection instruments and procedures | 27 |
| | 3.4 | Methods of data analysis | 27 |
| 4. | **RESULTS AND DISCUSSION** | | 29 |
| | 4.1 | Demographic Characteristics of the Respondents | 29 |
| | 4.2 | The Actual Operation of PHEIs in terms of Improving Access and Providing Relevant and Quality Education | 31 |
| | 4.3 | Government regulatory framework related to PHEIs | 45 |
| | 4.4 | Public-private partnerships | 53 |
| | 4.5 | Employers' Satisfaction with the Performance of | 55 |

|   |     | Graduates from PHEIs |    |
|---|-----|----------------------|----|
|   | 4.6 | Opportunities and Challenges of PHEIs | 56 |
|   | 4.7 | Discussion of the major findings | 59 |
| **5.** | | **CONCLUDING REMARKS AND RECOMMENDATIONS** | 62 |
|   | 5.1 | Concluding remarks | 62 |
|   | 5.2 | Recommendations | 63 |
| 6 | | **REFERENCES** | 67 |

# List of Abbreviations

| | |
|---|---|
| AEPHEIs | Association of Ethiopian Private Higher Education Institutions |
| E.C. | Ethiopian Calendar |
| EPHEIs | Ethiopian Private Higher Education Institutions |
| ETP | Education and Training Policy |
| ETQAA | Education and Training Quality Assurance Agency |
| FDRE | Federal Democratic Republic of Ethiopia |
| FPPP | Forum for Public-Private Partnership |
| HE | Higher Education |
| HEIs | Higher Education Institutions |
| HEP | Higher Education Proclamation |
| HERQA | Higher Education Relevance and Quality Agency |
| MoE | Ministry of Education |
| MoFED | Ministry of Finance and Economic Development |
| OECD | Organization for Economic Cooperation and Development |
| PHEIs | Private Higher Education Institutions |
| PIL | Private Institution Leader |
| PUL | Public University Leader |
| REBs | Regional Education Bureaus |
| SMUC | St. Mary's University College |
| SPSS | Statistical Package for Social Sciences |
| TVET | Technical Vocational Education and Training |
| UNISA | University of South Africa |

# List of Tables and Figure

|  |  | Page |
|---|---|---|
| 1. | Sample PHEIs by location and questionnaires collected from respondents | 26 |
| 2. | Demographic characteristics of the sample respondents | 29 |
| 3. | Respondents' opinion regarding the contribution, relevance and quality of programs in PHEIs | 32 |
| 4. | Share of undergraduate student enrollment in PHEIs (Regular, Evening, Kiremt, Distance) across five years* | 33 |
| 5. | Respondents' satisfaction with the relevance and quality of education offered by PHEIs | 34 |
| 6. | Types of study programs offered by PHEIs (2004/05-2008/09)* | 35 |
| 7. | Instructors' satisfaction with the commitment of their institution | 38 |
| 8. | Respondents' satisfaction with the availability and adequacy of resources | 39 |
| 9. | Respondents' ratings on the balance between business motive and stakeholders' expectations | 40 |
| 10. | Qualification mix of full time Ethiopian academic staff for some PHEIs (2010/11)* | 44 |
| 11. | Instructors' opinion about regulatory frameworks related to PHEIs | 46 |
| 12. | Respondents' ratings on the status of public-private partnerships | 54 |// 
| **Figure** | | |
| 1. | Conceptual framework of the study | 22 |

# Acknowledgement

The research team would like to extend its utmost gratitude to the Forum for Social Studies (FSS) for providing financial support and facilitating the research undertaking. Special thanks also go to the Institute of Educational Research (IER), Addis Ababa University, for its contribution in identifying members of the research team and providing them with the necessary administrative support. Moreover, our warmest gratitude is extended to those officials in the MoE, HERQA/ETQAA, senior managers of both private and public HEIs, the representative of the AEPHEIs, employers, parents, instructors, current students and graduates of sample PHEIs who contributed to the success of the research by providing the necessary information and expediting the data collection process.

# Abstract

The main purpose of this study was to explore current issues surrounding Ethiopian private higher education institutions (PHEIs) and assess the impact of regulatory practices on the smooth operation of PHEIs. To this effect, a blend of quantitative and qualitative research methods was used. The study was conducted in 16 PHEIs found in different parts of the country. The sample respondents were 135 instructors, 314 students, 72 graduates who have completed their studies, 16 senior managers of the sample PHEIs, and 6 public universities. Besides, 30 parents, 10 employers and concerned officials of the MoE, HERQA/ETQAA, and a representative of the PHEIs' Association were included in the sample. Information was solicited from the sample respondents through questionnaires and interviews. Appropriate statistical tools were used for data analysis. The findings of the study revealed that PHEIs are making significant contribution towards increasing access to higher education and creating employment opportunities. However, there were concerns among stakeholders on the quality of education provided by PHEIs. The application of government regulatory frameworks was also found to be more stringent on PHEIs than on their counterparts in the public sector. In general, the study established that due to frequent and unexpected changes in the implementation of the regulatory policy and laws, PHEIs could not run their programs smoothly and satisfy the needs of their stakeholders. Hence, it was recommended that a robust and comprehensive regulatory framework and autonomous implementing agency that equally serves the public and private providers be put in place so as to assure and enhance the provision of relevant and quality higher education in both private and public HEIs of the country.

**Key words**: accreditation, business, policy, quality, relevance, stakeholders

# Current Issues in Ethiopian Private Higher Education Institutions: Opportunities and Challenges

## 1. Introduction
### 1.1 Background of the Study

The provision of private higher education has expanded exponentially in many countries across the globe over the last decade. The increasing demand for higher education coupled with inadequate government funding, the rise of market ideology and competitiveness are considered as the major deriving forces for the emergence and growth of the private higher education sector in the world. These days the private higher education sector is seen as a means of expanding access to higher education in many countries. It is estimated that approximately 30 percent of global higher education enrolments are now in private sector institutions, and in some developing countries like the Philippines, Indonesia, Brazil, Jordan, and Chile; 35 to 80 percent of higher education provision is covered by the private sector institutions (Ashcroft 2007). However, Africa in general and Sub-Saharan Africa in particular has been late to modern private higher education, although breakthroughs came in the 1980s and 1990s in the region (Bjarnason, et. al. 2009).

The market-friendly reforms initiated under the structural adjustment programs, the deregulation policies and the fiscal incapacity of the state to expand higher education through public universities, the inability of public universities to respond immediately to household demand for employment-oriented courses created a conducive environment for the emergence and expansion of private higher education in Africa since the end of the 20$^{th}$ century (Varghese, 2004). As a result, many African countries have initiated reform and change in their higher education systems that encourage the growth and expansion of private higher education and Ethiopia is not an exception.

In Ethiopia, the higher education system has exhibited significant change since the adoption of the 1994 Education and Training Policy (ETP). Institutional expansion and diversification of the systems (and programs) are some of the major changes. The reform has considered the establishment of private higher education institutions (PHEIs) as one strategy to enhance the contribution of the sector towards the nation's development agenda. Consequently, many private higher education institutions have flourished over the past thirteen years. As the recent statistical abstract of the Ministry of Education indicates, there are about eighty six higher education institutions in the country that offer training via regular, evening, summer and distance modalities. The undergraduate student enrolment in both public and private higher education institutions is 447,693. Out of this, the non-governmental higher education institutions (PHEIs included) enrol approximately 78,439 students, which accounts for 17.5 % of the total enrolment (MoE 2011).

This shows that the private sector is making significant contribution to bridging the gap between the increasing demand for and the supply of higher education by the government. Some of the notable contributions private higher education institutions have made include:

- Creating access to higher education to citizens who couldn't join public HEIs.

- Helping the government by reducing the cost it needs for producing knowledgeable and skilled human resources. According to the Ministry of Information (cited in the Reporter Newsletter, October 11, 2009, 46), PHEIs have created opportunities to citizens to be employed in different sectors. The report published in 2008 by the Ministry of Information indicated that PHEIs have created opportunities to 71,800 fulltime and 21,058 part-time employments. The same source acknowledges that the projects undertaken on education by the private education sector between 1991 and 2006/07 showed a registered capital of Birr 10.33 billion investment, which is a significant contribution of the sector towards the economic development of the country.

- Moreover, the PHEIs have made efforts to increase female enrolment, which is in line with the government's efforts to enhance female participation in higher education institutions. More than 50% of the students participation rate in these institutions is that of females.

- Furthermore, these institutions offer scholarships to needy groups who have diverse problems like those who live with HIV/AIDS and are unable to pay tuition fees.

According to the third Education Sector Development Program (ESDP III), higher education is envisioned to expand rapidly between 2005 and 2011; the private higher education sector is expected to enroll 45,000 to 50,000 students at the end of 2011 academic year (Nwuke, 2008, 90). As Damtew (2005,1) pointed out, in private institutions "the enrollment rate appears to have been climbing rapidly for several years; but the pace has now moderated, and in a few cases a decline has been reported". This suggests that the private provision of higher education in Ethiopia has been contributing its share towards societal, political, and economic development of the country by increasing access to higher education opportunities.

Regarding the legal framework, both public and private higher education institutions are required to operate under the same higher education proclamation (No. 351/2003), which was revised in 2009 (No. 650/2009). The autonomy, governance and accountability of higher education institutions regarding the opening and provision of their educational programs are clearly stipulated in this proclamation. Accordingly, PHEIs are not allowed to operate without licenses from a recognized body in the Ministry of Education. The government's relationship with PHEIs is centred in regulatory policies that range from a decision to allow a private provider to plan a program up to the approval and regular monitoring of programs.

However, the implementation of the regulatory frameworks, including laws, directives, and guidelines specifically within the context of PHEIs, has become a point of heated debate among all stakeholders. Thus, this study intends to explore the impact of the regulatory practices and other related factors on the operation of PHEIs in the country.

## 1.2 Statement of the Problem

Provision of education by private institutions at a tertiary level in Ethiopia is relatively new but considerably growing. The establishment of PHEIs is a response to the increasing demand for access to higher education, which is grounded in the country's economic, societal and political development agenda. Even though this establishment is demand-driven, PHEIs seem to have a complex relationship with the government. The various policy documents of the government offer good grounds in guiding and facilitating the establishment of PHEIs. However, the PHEIs repeatedly complain about the unfairness of the government in different media.

They even have gone on accusing the government for using the public media to report unbalanced and unfair information about the PHEIs. A recently conducted study on this issue asserted that "the majority of the PHEIs are dissatisfied with the consistency and amount of news and /or feature stories coverage given to them" (Hailemarkos, 2006, 128).

Most of the PHEIs agree that, compared to the public HEIs, the government is too stringent on them concerning accreditation, quality assurance practices, etc; and issues unexpected directives and guidelines specifically for PHEIs time and again. For instance, in his comparative analysis of country laws, Wondwossen

(2005) concluded that the Ethiopian Higher Education proclamation lacks articles concerning reward and support for PHEIs, except land. The author also noted some limitations of the proclamation in terms of the procedures of accreditation and closure of PHEIs. In this connection, the PHEIs decry the government for changing students' admission and training guidelines without consulting them and failing to give due attention that such changes may have on these institutions.

Similarly, when the government plans and decides annual enrolment rate and criteria of the HEIs for a given year, it does not usually consider PHEIs, which have important contributions towards the development of the country's skilled and knowledgeable human resources. Some of the other grudges of the PHEIs as presented by the Association of Ethiopian Private Higher Education Institutions/AEPHEIs in the Reporter Newsletter (October 11,2009) read as follows:

> Contrary to the country's education policy and strategy, participation of PHEIs towards the development of skilled and knowledgeable human resources using distance mode of education is denied as of 2009/10. Similarly, three years back, the government declared that teacher education programs should only be run by public HEIs. Together with this, a decision was made not to hire graduates who studied teacher education programs in PHEIs. Unlike the regulatory policy and laws, it is believed that there is the use of double standards by the government, which is specifically more stringent on the PHEIs than the public HEIs. It was also underlined that the government erodes the autonomy of the PHEIs by interfering with the daily administrative activities of these institutions (p, 46).

On the government side, ensuring quality and relevance of the educational programs provided by PHEIs is the main concern. Thus, PHEIs are expected to demonstrate to their stakeholders that they are providing relevant and quality education. This requires the need to put in place and implement regulatory systems by the government that provide the right balance between protecting the public interest and encouraging the smooth operation of PHEIs. This means that PHEIs are subject to sanctions in case of providing poor quality training programs. To this effect, the Higher Education Relevance and Quality Agency (HERQA) has carried out a series of institutional quality audits in many of the PHEIs over the last three years. For example, the institutional quality audit reports of Unity University College, St. Mary's University College, Admas University College, City University College, and Royal University College indicate that although the institutions have some good practices, such as establishing important committees and offices to support their programs, conducting student satisfaction surveys, etc., they have major limitations in staff profile, teaching and assessment methods, embedding planned program of regular curriculum reviews, providing their students with the necessary support and guidance, conducting stakeholders' satisfaction surveys and establishing a fully-functional and integrated quality assurance system (HERQA, 2009).

These quality audit reports indicate that there is a concern on the part of stakeholders, especially HERQA, regarding the quality and relevance of education provided by PHEIs. In this connection, restrictions are imposed on PHEIs in running teacher education and law training programs based on the government's concern with the deteriorating quality of graduates of the PHEIs in these fields of study. The abovementioned issues thus call for an empirically based research so as to uncover the situation in which PHEIs are operating by focussing on the impact of regulatory practices on the operation of PHEIs as compared to public HEIs, the balance between PHEIs' business motives and stakeholders' needs, status of public-private partnership, employers' satisfaction with the performance of PHEIs' graduates, and the challenges that PHEIs encountered. Accordingly, this study attempted to address the following research questions.

1. How are the PHEIs addressing the need for increased access to higher education vis-à-vis the higher education proclamation?
2. How are the government regulatory frameworks affecting PHEIs compared to the public HEIs in Ethiopia? How do the PHEIs respond to requirements of the regulatory frameworks?
3. What is the status of public-private partnership in Ethiopian higher education? Is there a healthy relationship between the government and owners of PHEIs regarding the provision of higher education in the country?
4. To what extent are employers satisfied with the performance of graduates from PHEIs?
5. What are the opportunities and major challenges of PHEIs in Ethiopia?

## 1.3 Objectives of the Study

The major objective of this study is to explore the impact of regulatory practices on the operation of PHEIs and identify the opportunities as well as major challenges of PHEIs. More specifically, the study intends to:

- Examine the role of PHEIs in addressing the need for increased access to higher education,

- uncover the extent to which government regulatory frameworks are affecting the smooth operation of PHEIs compared to public HEIs in Ethiopia,
- explore the status of public-private partnership in Ethiopian higher education,
- examine the level of employers' perceived satisfaction with the performance of graduates from PHEIs,
- identify the opportunities that encourage and/or the major challenges that hinder the smooth operation of PHEIs in the country.

## 1.4 Scope of the study

This study didn't intend to evaluate the effectiveness of the teaching-learning process, governance, financial management, staff utilization, etc. of PHEIs. It rather attempts to examine the role of PHEIs in addressing the demand for higher education, the impact of regulatory practices on the operation of PHEIs as compared to public ones, the status of public-private partnership, employers' satisfaction with the performance of PHEIs' graduates, and the opportunities as well as the major challenges of PHEIs.

## 2. Conceptual and Theoretical Framework

This section presents the literature on the conceptual and theoretical issues of private higher education in a global context. It begins with a brief overview of the forces that derive privatization in higher education followed by the different conceptualizations of PHEIs, public-private partnerships and the factors that influence the behavior and functioning of private higher education institutions. Then, the conceptual framework of the study is illustrated followed by a brief discussion on the PHEIs context in Ethiopia.

### 2.1. The Forces that Underlie Privatization in Higher Education

Higher education systems worldwide have been heavily affected by a combination of demographic, political and socio-economic pressures that resulted in a variety of reforms. The key elements driving reform and change in world-wide higher education systems include: the increasing social demand, the rise of knowledge economy, globalization and competition within the international economy, the application of communication and information technologies and the changed funding arrangements for higher education.

In response to the pressing demands for reform and change, policies and strategies of decentralization, privatization and marketization are becoming increasingly popular in many higher education systems (Mok & Lee, 2001). The implementation of such reform initiatives has resulted in the expansion, massification and diversification as well as change in the structure, content and delivery systems of higher education across many countries. It is often considered that diversity in higher education is best ensured by the free play of market forces (Teixeira & Amaral, 2001). Market forces in turn are characterized by competition, efficiency and effectiveness. The common and recurring strategies to introduce market or quasi-market structures into higher education are to call for its privatization, although privatization can, and does, take a variety of forms (Teixeira & Amaral, 2001).

Since the late 1970s, political support has grown across the world for the idea that the role of the private sector in higher education, notably in its funding, should be increased significantly (Teixeira & Amaral 2001). As noted by LaRocques (2008), democratization or massification of higher education, inability of the public sector to meet the increasing demands for higher education; favorable regulatory reform, growth in private economy fueling demand for new more job oriented skills, and growing diversity of student background are the main reasons/driving forces for the growth of private higher education in many developed countries.

A similar pattern can be observed concerning the emergence and development of PHEIs in Africa. To mention some, Kenya has led the establishment of PHEIS since the early 1990s, and it was soon joined by Benin, Senegal, Tanzania, Uganda, Ghana, Mozambique and Cameroon (Varghese, 2006). Nigeria had also a prolonged history of legislating higher education in favor of PHEIs since the 1990s. The main reasons that drive the emergence of PHEIs in Africa, among other things, include: 1) the inability of the public sector to satisfy the growing social demand for higher education; 2) the changing political view of large scale public subsides to social sectors; 3) the changes in demands for courses and subjects of study, and the inability of the public sector to address such demands; 4) the perceived inefficiency of the public sector and promotion of the private sector for its efficiency, and 5) the transition from state planning to market forces (Varghese, 2004). Ethiopia is no exception in this regard.

The increasing attention given to the importance of private higher education has led to the fast growth of the sector across many countries over the past years. For example, in Japan, South Korea, Taiwan and the Philippines; private higher education caters for more than 70 percent; in India and Malaysia more than 30 percent, in Mainland China; Thailand and Vietnam more than 15 percent; in Sub-Saharan Africa, it caters for about 10 percent; in post-communist countries for about 30 percent, whereas in Latin America, it is about 40 percent (Gupta, 2008). In Ethiopia, the undergraduate enrolment in private higher education institutions accounts for 17.5% of the total undergraduate enrolment in 2011 (MoE, 2011), which is higher than the Sub-Saharan Africa average.

The main driving forces for the emergence and rapid growth of private higher education in Ethiopia include:

- the degree of unmet demand for higher education that had arisen as a consequence of the decades-long civil war;
- the liberal economic and social policies adopted by the present government soon after it came to power in 1991;
- the bulge in secondary enrolments and the consequent urgent need to expand access to higher education, which is a result of the intensified efforts being made to meet the Millennium Development Goals;
- relevance of the courses and programs offered to the country's changing labor market that demands for technical and professional skills;
- the growth per capita income in recent years, which expands the higher education consumption of the populace;

- and the introduction of cost sharing in the public higher education that increases the relative attractiveness of private higher education (Nwuke, 2008).

The foregoing discussions seem to suggest that the driving forces for the emergence of private higher education in Ethiopia align with the worldwide experience of privatization. The surge of demand for higher education is most commonly articulated as the major cause for the emergence of the private sector across many countries, whether in Africa or else where in the world.

## 2.2 Conceptualizing Privatization of Higher Education

Generally, privatization implies the application of market principles in the operation and management of higher education institutions (both private and public), and private higher education institution implies the rise of the non-state sector in the knowledge realm (Gupta, 2008). Privatization can take different forms, which includes privatization of student services; privatization as cost sharing through loan/scholarship schemes; privatization through education vouchers that permit parents to choose the colleges or universities for their children based on the payment provided by the state; privatization through the corporatization of universities, and the private management of public higher education (Varghese, 2006). Private higher education institution may include state-supported or non-profit or for-profit private institutions (Varghese, 2004). State-supported private institutions receive minimal or maximum funding support from the government. Non-profit private institutions are self-financing institutions that are owned by trusts and religious groups and rely heavily on endowments and fees collected from students. For profit private higher education institutions are, by design, seen as institutions established to make profit.

As Geiger (1987) noted, the amount and kind of higher education provided by government is the single most important determinant of the size and character of private higher education in each national system. According to Geiger, private higher education institutions are classified into three basic types/forms as follows:

***Type one -mass private and restricted public sectors*** - is a higher education system, which is dominated by massive private sector with restricted public sectors. The driving force behind mass private sectors is private demand for higher education. This type has arisen in countries where the provision of public higher education has been limited to relatively few institutions of generally high academic standing. This type is characterized by the accommodation of a large proportion of students in low-cost, low-quality institutions created to absorb excess demand with inadequate resources and part-time staff. Private institutions in mass private sectors are most heavily dependent upon student tuition. Examples of countries classified under this category include Japan, the Philippines, South Korea, Brazil, Columbia, and to some extent Indonesia (Geiger, 1988).

***Type two--parallel public and private sectors --*** is a parallel system in which both the private and public sectors play a role in providing education services. This type is characterized by a symmetrical relationship of private and public sectors, and requires three conditions: a) the existence of 'legitimate' cultural groups whose interests are represented in the polity; b) a single high national standard for university degrees; and c) extensive government subsidization of private institutions in order to equalize conditions with the public sector (Zha, 2006). This includes full state funding for private universities. U.S.A, Latin America, Belgium, the Netherlands, New Zealand, and Hong Kong are examples in this regard.

***Type three--comprehensive public & peripheral private sectors--*** refers to the peripheral private sector in which the private sector plays a very limited role. Peripheral private sectors emerge to serve purposes not acknowledged by the state, where public sectors are designed to fulfill all of the recognized need for higher education (Zha, 2006). Government support for higher education is concentrated in the comprehensive public sector. Peripheral private sector institutions are unlikely to have the resources to compete academically with public sector institutions. Geiger maintains that "these factors make peripheral private institutions among the most private in higher education." Examples under this category include Sweden, Mexico, Germany, China and almost all African countries (e.g., Cameroon, Ghana, Kenya, Nigeria, Senegal, South Africa, Tanzania, Uganda, and Zimbabwe, etc).

The preceding discussion indicates that the private higher education sector in Africa is characterized by the third type of privatization in Geiger's classification. This suggests that the higher education systems of many countries including Africa are characterized by a monopoly of public universities, except in some East Asian and Latin American countries. This poses a question as to whether the present characteristics of the higher education system of African countries with peripheral private sector address the felt need to improve the present low higher education participation rate in the continent.

## 2.3 The Public-Private Partnerships

Traditionally, discussions on the public-private distinctions in higher education were rooted in the perspectives of political economy and liberal political philosophy. Both perspectives treat public and private as mutually exclusive concepts, in which the economic notion associates 'public' with not–a natural market and the political philosophy associates 'public' with government or state (Marginson, 2007). From the neo-classical economics point of view, for the most part, higher education is a natural private good and should be marketized, whereas in liberal political philosophy higher education is a public good (Marginson, 2007). The economics view tends to downplay the potential for collective goods in higher education and the liberal political philosophy underestimates the role of markets. These two perspectives are criticized for their dualistic nature, i.e. treating public and private as mutually exclusive. Considering the flaws contained in the two perspectives, Marginson (2007) argued as follows.

> Sectors, such as higher education, are intrinsically neither public nor private. They can go either way. They can produce predominantly private goods, or predominantly public goods, or achieve an (unstable) balance between them. The mix of public and private goods is determined by public policy... the emphasis is on private or public goods is not determined by the 'intrinsic nature' of the good (including services) but is a prior policy decision (p, 315).

The author further noted that 'the ownership of higher education can be exclusively public, or mixed, or exclusively private. But almost everywhere in the world, what is produced is a variable mixed of public and private goods. To the extent that public/private is a positive sum, one can augment the other.' This suggests that both state and private sector institutions produce public and private goods, and both sectors are accessible to policy, i.e., ownership and policies are only two of the inputs that determine higher education.

Moreover, private and public goods are particular rather than universal attributes and their dynamics are different, i.e., in certain circumstances they augment each other, while in other circumstances the relationship is either/or (Marginson, 2007). Higher education has usually been referred to as a public or quasi-public good on the one hand mainly because of the externalities it yields to society. On the other hand, higher education is not a public good seeing that marginal cost of its provision to an additional individual is not zero and it is not difficult to exclude a person from consuming it. Individualized status benefits or positional goods, such as securing superior incomes and social standing, are the main private goods produced in higher education, whereas knowledge, collective literacy and common culture are classic public goods in higher education.

Marketization is normally associated with enhancement of the role of private goods relative to public goods. As argued by Marginson (2007), equitable access tends to be underprovided in markets because the effects of private capacity to pay and exclusive behavior by producers are to create absolute barriers to entry, and/or to stratify opportunity between high cost, high value and low cost, low value institutions. Due to this reason, many countries across the world use the provision of an equitable structure of opportunity as one of the principal drivers of government regulation, financing and higher education provision.

Studies indicate that, the public sector has traditionally enjoyed a near monopoly of higher education in most countries of the world until the 1990s, except for some East Asian and Latin American nations, where private universities have long been established (Bjarnason et al., 2009). This situation was changed in the early years, and private higher education has now become the most dynamic segment of higher education that accounts for a significant share of institutions and student enrolment across many countries. In many countries, encouraging the private sector is seen as the only means of expanding access to higher education when the state is confronted with fiscal facilities (ibid).

In most cases, the private sector does not receive funding from the government and, in any case, does not rely on state funding for its growth and expansion (Bjarnason et al., 2009). The experience of African countries, such as Kenya, South Africa, and Uganda, also indicates that both privatization of public institutions and the growth of the private sector were ineffective.

These trends have brought the need for public-private partnerships in the higher education systems of many countries. Public-private partnership reflects the interplay between the state and the market, and at the macro-systemic level, public–private partnership means the inclusion of the private sector as part of the nation's strategic development of higher education (Bjarnason et al., 2009). The relationship between public and private higher education institutions could be characterized by competition; complimentarity or a combination of both. In this connection, Chang Da (2007) noted the following:

> In the competitive relationship, both public and private institutions have similar characteristics and compete for a homogeneous group of students. In the complimentarity relationship, the public institution's fee is subsidized by government and all students prefer to join this institution to benefit from the low tuition fee. However, the public institution has limited capacity. Consequently, those who fail to do so will seek tertiary education in the private institution (p,3).

Whatever the relationship between public and private institutions, the important question here is how can the public interest be served? As argued by Dill (2005), the public interest is best served by policies, which assure that all publicly subsidized institutions of higher education -- whether they are public, private not-for profit, or private for-profit -- provide human capital to the society in as efficient and equitable a manner as possible. This has an implication on the need to develop reliable alliances between the public and private sectors based on well-established regulatory frameworks and policies. As Bjarnason et al. (2009) noted, the distrust and competition between these two sectors should be replaced by mutual trust and cooperation in order to contribute to higher education and national development. The authors further argue that successful public-private partnership entails the following measures:

1. Honoring the private sector as a respectable partner that includes appreciating the advantage of the private sector over the public sector; fully exploiting the strengths of the market; and learning from the private sector in terms of efficiencies,

2. Formulating an inclusive policy framework where the private sector has an active role to play. This could include creating the necessary legislation to legitimize the position of private institutions; providing government direct subsidy to students and teachers, generally in the form of student loans but sometimes as subsidies to qualified teachers, as in Indonesia; and providing a level playing field for the private institutions to receive competitive grants, that is, for research grants or matching grants for donations. In many countries, private sector higher education receives substantial funding and grants from the state. For example, Tilak (1991 cited in Bjarnason et al. 2009) discovered that in most developed countries, state subsidies cover more than 90% of the recurrent expenditure of private institutions and that, in Sweden and Canada, the government provides the capital needs for private institutions. Similarly, implicit subsidies or indirect government support is an important source of funding for private universities in the USA.

3. Adopting a positive attitude and creating space in the higher education landscape so that the private sector can play a significant role. This could mean facilitating and developing private institutions as a major thrust in higher education expansion; facilitating the establishment and development of elite institutions in the private sector. For example, like in Hong Kong (China), Singapore, and the United Kingdom where there are matching funds programs; introducing elements in the tax system so as to create incentives for private sector participation in higher education; and actively creating innovative ways to involve the private sector.

4. Involving the private sector in higher education policy formulation. This could involve creating a platform for policy dialogue between the government and the private sector representatives. It could also mean

inclusion of the representatives from private institutions in national higher education policy-making bodies.

5. Changing the paradigms in governance and administration in order to positively derive benefits from the market. This would mean moving away from the civil service ideology, where procedures, rules and regulations prevail; creating concepts and systems of accountability alternative to public sector administration; and tolerating temporary and minor chaos due to the market, to the same extent as tolerating bureaucracy.

The points mentioned above refer to the ideal conditions necessary for successful public-private partnership in any country. However, it is unusual to find all of these conditions in place across many countries, especially in the developing world like Africa. As indicated earlier, the higher education system of many African countries is characterized by a peripheral private higher education system. In this context, there are some examples of public-private partnerships in some African countries. In Botswana, government subsidies to the private institutions by way of land allocation or the provision of capital for construction necessary for the initial operation of the institution, is a good example of public-private partnership. As noted by Bjarnason et al. (2009), Botswana is establishing a new university on a public-private partnership basis to address the issue of scarce public resources. In this model, the state will provide substantial funding for capital expenditure while the private sector will be responsible for operational expenditure. A similar venture is being created in Zambia at Mulungushi University.

The issues discussed in this section suggest that a balanced public-private partnership is necessary to ensure the significant role of the private higher education sector in boosting access and quality of higher education. This has an implication for developing countries like Ethiopia where the participation rate of their higher education is still very low compared to other East Asian and OECD countries, and there is a pressing demand for expansion of access to higher education.

## 2.4. Factors Affecting the Behavior and Functioning of PHEIs

Private higher education institutions are not free from their environmental influences. They are subject to both external and internal environmental influences. Some of the possible factors that influence the operation of private higher education institutions include: market; government regulatory policy and laws; relevance and quality of the education provided by the private sector;

socio-economic and demographic aspects; etc. A brief description of these factors is presented below.

## Market

The market is seen as a mechanism through which the diverse and multitudinous wants of consumers are met, and it is invariably presented as a source of diversity in educational provision (Middleton, 2000). Market in the higher education context includes the education market and labor market. The education market refers to the potential demand for higher education and labor market refers to the absorptive capacity of the economy for graduates of HEIs in terms of employment. The education market of higher education depends on many factors. One of the factors is demographic. The demand for higher education, which is mostly grounded in population growth of a country, influences the education market of private higher education. In Africa, for example, the increasing demand for higher education due to the expansion of primary and secondary education has encouraged the establishment of private higher education since the 1990s (Varghese, 2006). This is, however, not the case in many OECD countries, where many of these countries are affected by reductions in enrolments of the traditional 18-25 year old student age group (OECD, 2006).

Demand for higher education by itself may not be sufficient; the ability of the parents and students to pay for higher education also influences the growth of private providers. In the Ethiopian context, the population below poverty line is 38.7%, although the economy, on overage, grew at around 10% over the past few years with a real growth rate 11.1% in 2007; 11.6% in 2008 and 6.8% in 2009 (CIA, World Fact Book, 2010). Market also influences the behavior of private higher education institutions. This includes the degree of competition among private and public institutions for students, funding and grants. Underlying the market orientation of tertiary education is the ascendancy of, almost worldwide of market capitalism and the principles of neo-liberal economics (Johnstone, 1998).

According to Marginson (2007), a move to markets is normally associated with enhancement of the role of private goods relative to public goods. Concerning markets and public goods, the author further noted the following:

> Pro-market ideologies and policies tend to conceal the possibility and actuality of public goods from view. However, under-recognition and underproduction do not eliminate public goods altogether. Markets in higher education suggest the need to policies designed to enhance those public goods that markets create, and to compensate for those public goods that markets tend to suppress from view and in effect (Marginson 2007, p. 321).

In higher education systems such as Africa, where market forces have been largely absent, the trend to enhance the production of private goods through the installation of market mechanisms is beginning to appear. Whereas in systems such as USA, where inter-institutional competition and tuition charges have been the norm for some time, these factors are becoming more productive, more shaping of the social character of higher education (ibid). Markets are becoming important in expanding access to higher education. Market principles, however, have their own weaknesses. Markets require profits and this can crowd out important educational duties and opportunities in the areas of basic sciences and humanities, which are essential for national development (Bjarnason et al., 2009). It is argued that PHEIs should not be left to the vagaries of market forces. According to Bjarnason and associates (2009), markets are more reliable in ensuring efficiency than equity, while their role in ensuring quality is debatable. In this connection, the authors further noted that:

> An unregulated free market in higher education may lead to investments in the sectors by low-quality providers that adversely affect best interests of the ultimate consumers. There have been instances when fraudulent practices have come to light in which admission rule are relaxed, the evaluation process is distorted and examination processes are faked in different ways. It is easy to create a new university in name only, and there are many ill-informed and naïve potential students desperate for higher education who may sign up to study at a private institution without knowing its credentials and quality (pp71-72).

This suggests that the motive behind government regulation for PHEIs across many countries is the need to protect consumers from ill-practices and poor quality services, which could result from free market principles. In this regard, regulatory frameworks are necessary to ensure the balance between the business motive and relevance and quality of educational provisions of PHEIs. In the section that follows, an attempt is made to explore the motives and main elements of a government regulatory framework that are supposed to affect the operation and growth of PHEIs across different countries.

## Government Regulatory Framework

Differently from competitive markets that mainly respond to the supply and demand conditions, regulatory frameworks or institutional arrangements set by national governments serve as the principal factors in shaping the dynamics of both public and private sectors in higher education (Pachuashvili, 2009). The term regulation, according to Bjarnason et al. (2009), refers to all aspects of the government's relationship with the private sector; it begins with a decision to allow a private provider to plan or develop a campus, continues with the approval of programs, awards, the grant of operating incentives or the collection of tasks, and then includes regular monitoring together with the collection of information on financial and academic performance.

There are multiple mechanisms through which governments influence private higher education institutions. In this connection, Pachuashvili (2009, 37-38) reviewed and analyzed a list of eight governmental policies which are thought to affect private growth patterns in most significant ways as follows.

1) *Legislative framework* is the most fundamental policy that either permits or proscribes the existence of privately provided education. It provides a statutory basis for the operation of PHEIs and clarifies their obligations as well their rights and entitlements. Some of the examples of countries which have recently passed legislation of this kind include Bulgaria, Cameroon, China, the Czech Republic, Ethiopia, Malaysia, the Russian federation, Thailand and Tunisia. Bangladesh and Sri Lanka are examples of countries without any legislation or clear statements of government policy for PHEIs.

2) *Regulative framework* includes licensing, quality control and associated regulations. The extent of state mandate and regulation will encourage or restrict private sector growth and distinctiveness. This involves clearly defined procedures for establishing new PHEIs, and a regular and effective external quality assurance that has the confidence of the private providers and can assure the general public about quality of provision. From among African countries, Ghana and Kenya can be considered as good examples in this regard. In Kenya, the regulation sets out three stages in the establishment of a private university and in obtaining the full recognition of the institution, namely 1) temporary recognition, pending registration, 2) registration as a university, permission to start teaching, and 3) full accreditation with the grant of an institutional charter allowing the university to award degrees. Many African countries including Ethiopia are following accreditation as an approach to regulate their PHEIs.

3) *Student aid policies include* portable student aid grants and student loans and can be designed in the way that facilitates or discourages student choice of private institutions. In developed countries, such as USA and Australia, private students are able to obtain the same grants and loans as public students (Bjarnason et al., 2009) whereas this is not the case in most of the developing world like Africa.

4) ***Direct state funding to private institutions*** includes financial support to private institutions (other than student aid), such as contracting with and direct appropriations to private institutions. This may include the ability of staff to bid for research funding on equal terms with state-funded academic staff, and policies on whether PHEIs can share in national academic infrastructure, such as a national ICT network. This policy can be viewed as the purchase of study slots at private institutions by the state according to students' choice of a university. In African countries, student fees continue to be the dominant source of income for the private universities (Varghese, 2006)

5) ***Tax policies*** – facilitate private institution development by means of tax exemption, deduction and credit policies. They also include tax exemptions on tuition fees for students and their families who pay them.

6) ***Governmental policies toward public institution tuition levels*** are a potent policy that can be used for creating competitive environment in which institutions operate. Whether governments ignore or regulate it strategically, the policy of pricing public higher education services has profound implications for private institutions

7) ***Governmental policies toward public institution expansion*** relates to governmental approach towards expanding access to higher education. Governmental policies can be designed so that they support enrollment growth in public sectors, encourage public sector privatization or assist private sector in accommodating rising demand for higher education (depending on whether the latter is viewed as an important means for achieving public purposes).

8) ***The Extent of private sector involvement in higher education planning process*** –governmental choice whether or not to include private higher sector representatives in this process has significant implications for the sector

According to Bjarnason and associates (2009), the main motive to regulate PHEIs by governments includes 1) protecting consumers; 2) allowing the collection and dissemination of information for decision-making by members of the public, which enables both students and their parents to make informed decisions regarding their choice of PHEIs; 3) ensuring that the public policy is based on accurate information about the activities of the private sector, and 4) monitoring the financial results of for-profit providers, since excessive profits could lead to the removal of any incentives or tax exemptions that might have been granted.

The authors concluded that where public policy favors private providers, the aim of a government must be to achieve a regulatory system that provides the right balance between protecting the public and encouraging private providers to invest. While a too rigorous regulatory system deters the development of the sector, a system that is too lax could lead to an avalanche of poor quality providers and degree mills. Public policies on PHEIs can vary depending on the motives of states. Zumeta (1997) identified three typologies: *laissez-faire, market-competitive* and *central-panning*.

In the *laissez-faire* policy posture, the state has little regard for private institutions as valued means for achieving its policy aims in higher education; no funds channeled to institutions; the governmental activity is minimal with respect to regulation, and private institutions have no role to play in a higher education planning process.

In the *central-panning* policy regime, by contrast, the state treats private sector as an integral part of its higher education system and employs private sector providers to play carefully planned roles to serve public purposes. The state becomes involved even in designing program configurations and assigning specific institutional roles to private universities to avoid duplication of missions through financial incentives, both in the form of direct appropriations to institutions and aid to their students.

In the *market-competitive* policy posture, the state plays a much more active role in private higher education development than is the case with the other two models. Under this model, governmental regulation is limited to quality control to a certain extent and addressing other market imperfections characteristic of the higher education sector. By using enrollment-driven funding, performance contracting arrangements and other market mechanisms, the state under this regime purposely creates a competitive environment in which both private and public institutions operate.

In countries such as England, France, Germany, Russia, Georgia, and Nigeria there are few rules and stipulations in terms of quality control and regulating private providers, whereas countries, such as New Zealand, Pennsylvania (USA), Latvia, Cyprus, Arab emirates, China, and many African countries (Kenya, Cameroon, Ghana, Uganda, South Africa, etc.), have robust and rigorous regulation for PHEIs, including relatively detailed guidelines for recognition. In most cases, the problems facing private providers in Africa have less to do with principles and more to do with how procedures are implemented (Bjarnason et al., 2009).

## *Relevance and Quality of Education*

The terms relevance and quality are subject to many interpretations. Relevance in higher education involves the bending of effort towards an immediate overriding goal, the perceived outcome and consequences, which promise advantage, utility, and in the widest sense, payback to those embarking on such a course (Neave, 2006). Ostensibly, relevance is a question of time due to the fact that yesterday's relevance of higher education too rapidly is held to mutate into today's irrelevance. What constitutes relevance today, according to Neave, is externally determined; and rests on a number of unpalatable and largely unjustified assumptions.

From the pragmatic point of view, relevance, like beauty lies in the eye of the beholder. The students, in this regard, are in a better position to know what skills they need to become employable, and the function of the PHEIs is, therefore, to provide what is needed, rather than to define relevance. Other stakeholders of PHEIs have also their own views of relevance. To the employers, relevance of education is related to the fitness of the knowledge and skills for job requirements; whereas the government views relevance of higher education in terms of its contribution to national socio-economic development. In this perspective, relevance is interpreted as the externalization of control exercised over academic productivity by systems of accountability, evaluation and performance (Neave, 2006), and quality assurance procedures are used to verify what the institution does is relevant. According to Gibbons (1998), relevance should be judged primarily in terms of outputs, the contribution that higher education makes to national economic performance and, through that, to the enhancement of the quality of life. This indicates that relevance and quality of education determine the relationship between higher education institutions, society and production.

Quality is a slippery concept that lacks a universally agreed definition. It is relative to the user of the term and the circumstances in which it is involved (Harvey & Green, 1993). Different stakeholders may have different thoughts about the meaning of quality. Vroeijenstijn (1992) suggested that all parties have an interest in quality, but not everyone has the same idea about it. Harvey & Green (1993) conceptualize quality in terms of five dimensions: quality as excellence; quality as consistency; quality as fitness for purpose; quality as value for money; and quality as transformation. In the Ethiopian context, HERQA conceptualizes quality as fitness for purpose as indicated in its reports. The meaning of quality from a variety of stakeholders' perspectives is considered important in the context of PHEIs. There are different stakeholders in PHEIs, including students, instructors, parents, employers, government and its funding agencies, and each of these stakeholders has a different view on quality, influenced by their own interest in higher education (Tam, 2001). In this connection, Reynolds (1990 cited in Tam 2001) noted that

> For example, to the committed scholar the quality of higher education is its ability to produce a steady flow of people with high intelligence and commitment to learning that will continue the process of transmission and advancement of knowledge. To the government, a high quality system is one that produces trained scientists, engineers, architects, doctors and so on in numbers judged to be required by society. To an industrialist, a high quality educational institution may be one that turns out graduates with wide-ranging, flexible minds, readily able to acquire skills, and adapt to new methods and needs (p,47)

The quality and relevance of the education provided by PHEIs varies within and across countries depending on the national legislation and regulatory frameworks. The quality of education in PHEIs is based on various factors, such as the level of infrastructural facilities, the quality of programs offered, the qualification level of teachers, the performance of students in their evaluation while in the university, and their performance in the labor market (Varghese, 2006). The relevance of education provided by PHEIs is related to the demands of the education and labor market, and their success depends upon their ability to respond quickly to such signals (ibid).

The range of courses offered by PHEIs depends on their capacity in terms of investment in infrastructure, facilities and teaching personnel. In most of the cases, private motivations and financial considerations determine the courses offered by PHEIs (Varghese, 2006). In Africa, the majority of the PHEIs offer market-friendly courses in areas of business administration, computer sciences, accounting, marketing, economics, and information communication technology that require limited investment in infrastructure and facilities (Varghese, 2006; Thaver, 2008). The extent to which the private higher education institutions comply with the quality and relevance requirements stipulated in government legislation and regulatory laws has implications on their operation and survival. In this study, how the relevance and quality of education provided by PHEIs influence their growth and smooth operation in the market is explored.

## *Socio-Economic and Demographic Factors*

There are many factors that shape private higher education across countries. One of the factors is demographic. The demand for higher education, which is mostly grounded in population growth of a country, influences the growth of private higher education. In Africa, for example, the increasing demand for higher education due to the expansion of primary and secondary education has encouraged the establishment of private higher education since the 1990s (Varghese, 2006). This is, however, not the case in many OECD countries, where many of these countries are affected by reductions in enrolments of the traditional 18-25 year old student age group (OECD, 2006).

Demand for higher education by itself may not be sufficient; the ability of the parents and students to pay for higher education also influences the growth of private providers. In the Ethiopian context, the population below poverty line is 38.7%, although the economy, on overage, grew at around 10% over the past few years with a real growth rate 11.1% in 2007; 11.6% in 2008 and 6.8% in 2009 (CIA World Fact Book, 2010). In this study, the demographic and socio-economic factors are assumed to influence the operation of PHEIs.

## 2.5. The Conceptual Framework of the Study

Based on the theoretical issues discussed in the preceding sections, the conceptual framework of the study is illustrated hereunder.

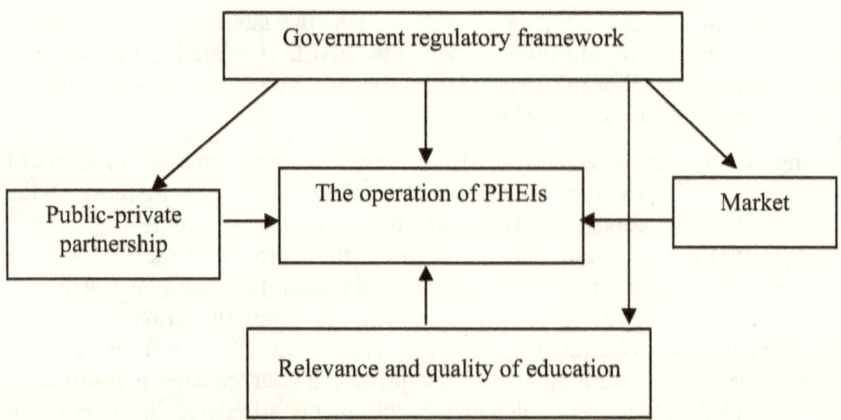

Figure1. Conceptual framework of the study

The arrows in the diagram indicate the direction of the influence among each variable and the growth and operation of PHEIs. The *government regulatory framework* in this study refers to the requirements set by the Higher Education Proclamation (No.650/2009) to govern both public and private HEIs and the policies, regulations and directives issued for the implementation of this proclamation as well as the accreditation, quality assurance guidelines and manuals set by HERQA. This framework is expected to influence relevance and quality of education, the market, the degree of public-private partnership, and thereby the overall operation of PHEIs. In this study, *relevance and quality* of the education provided by PHEIs refers to what the different stakeholders (students, parents, employers and government) conceive as appropriate and important education in terms of meeting the demands of the labor market, and this in turn influences the survival and operation of PHEIs. *Public-private partnership* includes the interplay between the state and the private sector as well as the joint venture of public and private HEIs for the strategic development of higher education in the country. The degree of partnership is expected to influence the smooth operation and contribution of PHEIs. *Market* is used to refer to the extent to which market principles are applied in the PHEIs, which include degree of competition within PHEIs and between public and private HEIs. The issue here is whether the rule of the game regarding market is equally applicable to both public and private HEIs, which is expected to influence the operation of the private sector.

## 2.6. The PHEIs' Context in Ethiopia

Prior to 1991, the Ethiopia higher education system was characterized by almost a monopoly of the public sector. Similar to other African countries, the government was the dominant provider of higher education during this time. Following the fall of the military regime, the government of Ethiopia has embarked on a number of reform initiatives including expansion, diversification, equity, and quality in the higher education sector since 1991. The reform initiatives were aimed at addressing the socio-economic demands for trained manpower and the changing context of global economic competitiveness. The implementation of such reform initiatives resulted in the introduction of private higher education.

In the Ethiopian context, private higher education is a recent phenomenon; it is almost fifteen years old. It caters for about 17.5% of the total higher education enrolment rate that is above the Sub Sahara African average (MOE 2011). There are 49 PHEIs that offer courses leading to a degree, which indicates the rapid expansion of the private higher education in Ethiopia. According to the Higher Education Proclamation (No.650/2009), private higher education institution means a non-public higher education institution established by one or more individual owners or by non-profit making associations, founded as co-operative society or commercial association, or higher education institution established abroad and operating in Ethiopia (FDRE, 2009). There is only one private university, while others are university colleges, colleges or institutes. The majority of the PHEIs are for-profit establishments that depend on tuition fees, whereas a few PHEIs are not-for profit institutions that are sponsored by non-government organizations, and religious institutions. The majority of the PHEIs in Ethiopia are owned by domestic providers, whereas some, such as the regional learning centre of the University of South Africa (UNISA) are owned by transnational organizations.

Ensuring strict compliance with the directives issued by the Ministry of Education on admission of students; ensuring the minimum curricula quality standards; performing regular annual self-evaluation; accrediting training programs, ensuring capable leadership and management, etc. are some of the responsibilities of PHEIs stipulated in the proclamation. Any PHEI is subject to accreditation every five years by the HERQA. The revised proclamation (No.650/2009) has abandoned the pre-accreditation registration requirements. This is considered by many as a positive step to encourage PHEIs open some of their programs and get approval if they fulfill the requirements set by the MoE. Regarding the benefits of the Proclamation, Wondwossen (2005) noted that the establishment of PHEIs in Ethiopia appears to be less bureaucratic but demanding. The proclamation gives room for the establishment of an institution with very limited capacity and with a similar status as that of well-established and highly organized PHEIs .

PHEIs in Ethiopia are playing vital roles in opening up opportunities for students who might not get a place in public universities; improving higher education access by enrolling about 17.5% of the undergraduate students, training individuals on market-responsive programs; opening up employment opportunities for professionals as well as non-professionals; motivating some private real-estate owners to build more apartments for rent; providing scholarship opportunities for disadvantage groups (especially females); and offering students an opportunity to choose their course of studies (Daniel, 2010).

Despite the apparent contributions of PHEIs in improving access to higher education and human resource development of the country, the quality and relevance of the courses offered by the private providers has become a point of debate among stakeholders. Some of the issues revolve around expansion, excessive focus on profit making and imbalance in accessibility (Daniel, 2010). Overall, many PHEIs are currently operating in the country share common features with those PHEIs established around the developing world.

## 3. Methodology of the Study

This section presents the data sources, sampling techniques and procedures, data collection instruments and procedures, and methods of data analysis. As indicated elsewhere in the text, this study dealt with the current issues surrounding the operation of Ethiopian PHEIs by focusing on the role of PHEIs in addressing the demand for higher education, the impact of regulatory framework and practices on the operation of PHEIs as compared to public HEIs, the status of public-private partnership, employers' satisfaction with PHEIs' graduates, and opportunities as well as challenges encountered. To this effect, a blend of qualitative and quantitative methods was used in the whole process of conducting the study. More specifically, the following procedures of qualitative and quantitative research methods were employed to select the sample institutions and respondents, and collect and analyze the data.

### 3.1 Data Sources

Both primary and secondary sources were consulted to obtain sufficient information for the study. Accordingly, first-hand information was collected from high-level officials of both private and public HEIs, instructors, students, and graduates of PHEIs. Besides, concerned officials in the MoE, HERQA, representative of the Association of EPHEIs, parents and employers were approached in order to document their opinions about PHEIs. Moreover, policy documents, institutional quality audit reports, relevant books, periodicals, research outputs and newspapers were duly reviewed.

### 3.2 Sampling Techniques and Procedures

According to the 2009 annual statistical abstract of the Ministry of Education, there were about fifty one accredited and reporting non-governmental higher education institutions in the country that offer training via regular, evening, summer and distance modalities. Out of these, sixteen private PHEIs (about 31 %) were selected on the basis of stratified random and purposive sampling techniques. The bases for stratification were: accreditation status, institution type (for-profit private, and non-profit private and/or religion affiliated), program type/level, field of training and geographical location (See Table 1 for details). In addition to the sample PHEIs, six public HEIs, i.e. Addis Ababa, Ambo, Bahir Dar, Haramaya, Hawassa, and Mekelle Universities were included in the sample for their role in training students who graduated from PHEIs and providing part-time staff to the private institutions.

Concerning respondent sampling, ten instructors and twenty current students from each of the sample PHEIs were selected and included in the sample on the basis of stratified random sampling technique taking into account such variables as gender, program type and level of education for students and gender, qualification, academic rank and teaching experience for instructors. Besides, five graduates of each of the sample PHEIs were included in the sample by using snowball-sampling technique. As regards high-level officials of both private and public HEIs, they were included in the sample on the basis of availability sampling technique due to their manageable size. Concerned officials in the MoE, HERQA, and representative of the Association of EPHEIs were also purposively selected and requested to express their views on the issue under study.

In addition, thirty parents and ten employers were included in the sample on the basis of snowball and convenient sampling techniques respectively. All in all, the sample size includes 625 respondents drawn from various categories of the population.

The following table portrays the sample PHEIs by location and number of questionnaires collected from the three groups respondents.

*Table 1. Sample PHEIs by location and questionnaires collected from respondents*

| No. | Institutions | Address | 1 | 2 | 3 |
|---|---|---|---|---|---|
| 1 | Admas University College | AA | 6 | 19 | 5 |
| 2 | Alpha University College | AA | 12 | 20 | 5 |
| 3 | City University College | AA | 5 | 20 | 4 |
| 4 | St. Mary's University College | AA | 8 | 17 | 6 |
| 5 | Unity University | AA | 10 | 17 | 5 |
| 6 | Mekane Yesus Mgmt & Lead. College | AA | 9 | 18 | 4 |
| 7 | Alkan University College | Bahir Dar | 10 | 26 | 5 |
| 8 | Blue Nile College | Bahir Dar | 6 | 18 | 6 |
| 9 | Africa Beza University College | Awassa | 9 | 20 | 4 |
| 10 | Aleph College of Health Sciences | Awassa | 9 | 20 | 1 |
| 11 | Ambo Micro Business College | Ambo | 9 | 20 | 5 |
| 12 | Microlink IT College | Mekelle | 10 | 20 | 5 |
| 13 | Mekelle Institute of Technology | Mekelle | 8 | 19 | 2 |

| 14 | Sheba University College | Mekelle | 9 | 19 | 7 |
| 15 | Lucy College | DireDawa | 7 | 21 | 4 |
| 16 | Horn College | Harer | 8 | 20 | 4 |
| | **Total** | | **135** | **314** | **72** |

NOTES: 1=Instructors, 2=Current students, and 3= Graduates

## 3.3 Data Collection Instruments and Procedures

The instruments used for collecting the required information were questionnaires, interviews and documentary analysis. That is, questionnaires were developed and distributed to instructors, students, and graduates of PHEIs; whereas a series of interviews were held with the high-level officials of both private and public HEIs, such as Presidents and/or Vice Presidents, deans, and concerned officials in the MoE, HERQA, representative of the Association of EPHEIs, parents and employers. In order to ensure whether the instruments are free of ambiguity and irrelevant items, draft questionnaires and interview protocols were pilot-tested in two PHEIs that are not included in the sample institutions.

In accordance with the results of the pilot test, necessary revisions were made and more clarifications included in the questionnaires. Accordingly, from the questionnaire prepared for instructors, the rating scales of one item were changed from Very Poor…Very High to Strongly Disagree…Strongly Agree continuum. Two items, which ask instructors about employers' satisfaction, were found irrelevant and then cancelled. Similarly, from the questionnaire prepared for students, the rating scales of one item were changed from Very Poor…Very High to Strongly Disagree…Strongly Agree continuum, one item was replaced by another which asks respondents about their agreement/disagreement on the effect of government policies/ regulatory frameworks on the operation of PHEIs. From the questionnaire prepared for graduates, one item was found redundant and then cancelled. Hence, the total number of questions was reduced from 17 to 16. Moreover, analysis of policy documents, institutional quality audit reports, relevant books, periodicals, research outputs, newspaper reports was made to augment and substantiate the data collected through questionnaires and interview protocols.

## 3.4 Methods of Data Analysis

Once the necessary data were collected, the first step was cleaning and editing the data for possible inconsistencies and inaccuracies. Then, the data were entered into a computer with commercially available software, i.e. Statistical Package for Social Sciences/SPSS 14.0 for Windows. After the completion of the data entry, a further cleanup was made. The second step of the analysis stage was a preliminary analysis of the data, which involved tabulating the frequencies of each variable and summarizing relevant statistics. Here, frequency tables, cross tabs, and summary statistics were computed. This step was followed by the testing of the basic questions using Chi-square test, mean, and percentages. The existing differences between and among the response patterns of respondents were tested for statistical significance at 0.05 and 0.01 alpha levels. Apart from this, the data obtained from the interviews were analyzed qualitatively using narrative descriptions after proper transcription of the recorded data.

## 4. Results and Discussion

This section presents results of the analyses of both quantitative and qualitative data collected from the sample respondents and documents. It starts with a summary of the demographic characteristics of respondents, followed by results of data analyses on the actual operation of PHEIs in terms of improving access and providing relevant and quality education. Then, it presents the findings regarding government regulatory framework that governs the operation of PHEIs. Following this, the results on the status of public-private partnership, employers' satisfaction with the performance of graduates, and the challenges facing PHEIs are presented sequentially. The section culminates by presenting the discussion of the major findings.

### 4.1 Demographic Characteristics of the Respondents

As mentioned earlier, 160 instructors, 320 students, and 80 former graduates were selected from the sample PHEIs. Accordingly, 560 questionnaires were distributed out of which 521 (93.04%), i.e. 135 instructors, 314 students, and 72 graduates' questionnaires were completed and returned (See Table 1 for details). Majority of the respondents from students (61.8%), instructors (91.9%) and graduates (59.7%) are male. The majority of the student respondents were drawn from the third year and degree program track. Of the total sample of graduates of PHEIs, those who pursued diploma and first-degree programs constitute 47.2% and 44.4 % respectively. In terms of field of study, the majority of the graduates have studied Management related fields followed by Accounting, Computer & Information Science, and Clinical Nursing & Pharmacy that are assumed to attract the labor market.

*Table 2. Demographic characteristics of the sample respondents*

| Respondents | Variable | Level | Frequency | Percent |
|---|---|---|---|---|
| Students (N = 314) | Gender | Female | 113 | 36.0 |
| | | Male | 194 | 61.8 |
| | | No Response | 7 | 2.2 |
| | Program | Diploma | 122 | 38.9 |
| | | Degree | 186 | 59.2 |
| | | Others | 6 | 1.9 |
| | Year/level of education | First | 12 | 3.8 |
| | | Second | 11 | 3.5 |
| | | Third | 158 | 50.3 |
| | | Fourth | 34 | 10.8 |
| | | Fifth & above | 99 | 31.6 |

| | | | | |
|---|---|---|---|---|
| Instructors (N = 135) | Gender | Female | 11 | 8.1 |
| | | Male | 124 | 91.9 |
| | Qualification | Diploma | 7 | 5.2 |
| | | BA/BSc | 80 | 59.3 |
| | | MA/MSc | 39 | 28.9 |
| | | PhD | 3 | 2.2 |
| | | Others | 6 | 4.4 |
| | Academic Rank | Graduate Assistant | 16 | 11.9 |
| | | Assistant Lecturer | 46 | 34.1 |
| | | Lecturer | 52 | 38.5 |
| | | Assistant Professor or Above | 3 | 2.2 |
| | | Others | 18 | 13.3 |
| | Teaching Experience | 1-3 Years | 65 | 48.2 |
| | | 4-6 Years | 44 | 32.6 |
| | | 7-15 Years | 13 | 9.6 |
| | | No Response | 13 | 9.6 |
| Graduates (N = 72) | Gender | Female | 29 | 40.3 |
| | | Male | 43 | 59.7 |
| | Type of Program Pursued | Diploma | 34 | 47.2 |
| | | BA/BSc | 32 | 44.4 |
| | | Others | 6 | 8.4 |
| | Field of Study | Accounting | 24 | 33.3 |
| | | Clinical Nursing & pharmacy | 8 | 11.2 |
| | | Management related | 30 | 41.7 |
| | | Computer & Info. Science | 10 | 13.8 |

The data in Table 2 further disclose that except 10 (7.4%) of the instructors, with the majority of them (59.3 and 28.9 %) are first and second-degree holders respectively. This may cast doubt on the qualification mix of instructors or staff profile in the private HEIs. As per HERQA's requirement, half of the academic staff of private HEIs should be second-degree holders and the rest need to have PhDs (30%) and first degrees (20%). Apart from this, the academic rank of the sample instructors is also dominated by lecturers followed by assistant lecturers. The proportion of those sample instructors with the rank of assistant professor and above is negligible.

Regarding teaching experience, the majority (48.2% and 32.6%) of the sample instructors have one to three years and four to six years of teaching experience in

HEIs respectively. It is only 19.2 % of the instructors who have seven and above years of teaching experience. This may indicate the extent to which the PHEIs are dominated by junior staff.

## 4.2 The Actual Operation of PHEIs in terms of Improving Access and Providing Relevant and Quality Education

This section presents results of the analysis of both quantitative and qualitative data on how the PHEIs operate in terms of increasing access to higher education and meeting the need for relevant and quality higher education. Although there is no clear definition of relevance of study programs by HERQA, the 'appropriateness of the balance of subject knowledge and transferable skills' is indicated as a reference point for evaluating program relevance and curriculum (HERQA, 2006). A closer look at HERQA's document on the areas of focus for institutional quality audit shows that higher education institutions, including PHEIs, are expected to justify the relevance of their programs and to have robust procedures for curriculum design, approval and review, which involve external professionals and employers. Conducting need assessment is implicitly implied as a mechanism to explore the demands of the market in the HERQA's documents.

For the purpose of this study, considering what is implied in the HERQA's documents and the literature review section, relevance of study programs is conceived in terms of the extent to which graduates of the PHEIs are equipped with marketable and transferable knowledge and skills for either self-employment or employment in organizations. In this regard, it is assumed that students and their parents choose a study program because of their perception of the appropriateness of the program in gaining employment after graduation. Employers perceive relevance of the training programs in terms of employability of graduates-the extent to which the knowledge and skills gained by graduates fits the requirements of jobs in the market. To the government, study programs are relevant to the extent that they address the trained manpower needs of the country, and this is clearly stipulated in the recent 70 (in Science & Technology) and 30 (in Humanities) higher education graduate mix policy of the MoE. This suggests that the different stakeholders of PHEIs have different views about relevance of training programs.

Similarly, the meaning of quality is implied in the HERQA's institutional self-evaluation document that 'quality of a higher education institution and its programs' is judged against what the institution aims to achieve (its mission and vision) and should be based on sound evidence'(HERQA, 2006), which implies the meaning of quality as 'fitness for purpose'. Ostensibly, the different stakeholders of PHEIs may not have the same thought about quality. For the purpose of this study, the stakeholders' perspective and view of quality as fitness for purpose, which is embedded in meeting the trained manpower needs of the market, students, employers, parents, and the nation at large, is considered important for the analysis of data. The indicators used to evaluate quality in higher education institutions including PHEIs are the ten focus areas provided by HERQA, which include, among other things, infrastructure and learning resources; staff adequacy and qualification; student admission and support services; program relevance and curriculum; teaching and learning; and internal quality assurance.

Accordingly, the perceived relevance and quality of education provided by PHEIs is analyzed using data obtained from students, parents, instructors, employers (including their satisfaction) and government officials as well as documentary evidences. The extent to which the PHEIs maintain the balance between their business motive and meeting stakeholders' needs was also considered as an indicator of relevance and quality. Results of the analysis of the quantitative data on the relevance and quality of education and training provided by PHEIs and documentary evidences are presented in the subsequent tables.

Table 3. Respondents' opinion regarding the contribution, relevance and quality of programs in PHEIs

| Variables | Current students | | | Instructors | | |
|---|---|---|---|---|---|---|
| PHEIs are contributing towards | yes | Total | $\chi^2$ | Yes | Total | $\chi^2$ |
| Improving access to higher education | 272(88) | 308 | 422* | 129(96) | 134 | 238* |
| Providing quality education | 213(69) | 307 | 181* | 84(65) | 130 | 57.3* |
| PHEIS give emphasis to maintain the: | Agree | Total | $\chi^2$ | Agree | Total | $\chi^2$ |
| Relevance of their programs | 198(83) | 238 | 104.9* | 64(48) | 134 | 30.5* |
| Quality of their programs | 199(81) | 246 | 93.9* | 57(43) | 134 | 18.8* |

*P< 0.01. Note: Numbers in brackets are percentages

The results in Table 3 above show that the majority of both student and instructor respondents believe that PHEIs are contributing towards improving access to higher education and providing quality education. The $\chi^2$ tests for the difference in respondents' ratings are significant. Results of the analysis of documentary evidences also corroborate the findings regarding access to higher education (see Table 4 below).

Table 4. *Share of undergraduate student enrollment in PHEIs (Regular, Evening, Kiremt, Distance) across five years\**

| Year | Gov't (Public HEIS) | | Non-Gov't (PHEIs) | | Total | | % Non-Gov't (PHEIs) | |
|---|---|---|---|---|---|---|---|---|
| | T | %F | T | %F | T | F | T | F |
| 1997E.C /2004-05/ | 120,384 | 22.6 | 17,775 | 33.4 | 138,159 | 24.0 | 12.9 | 17.9 |
| 1998E.C /2005-06/ | 134,210 | 23.0 | 39,691 | 30.6 | 173,901 | 24.8 | 22.8 | 28.2 |
| 1999E.C /2006-07/ | 169,049 | 23.9 | 34,350 | 36.4 | 203,399 | 26.0 | 16.9 | 23.7 |
| 2000E.C /2007-08/ | 214,199 | 23.0 | 48,802 | 28.7 | 263,001 | 24.1 | 18.6 | 22.1 |
| 2001 E.C /2008-09/ | 254,192 | 27.6 | 54,900 | 35.6 | 309,092 | 29.1 | 17.8 | 21.7 |

\*SOURCE: Education Statistics Annual Abstracts (MoE, 2004/05-2008/09).

From the results in Table 4 above, we can observe that the share of undergraduate enrollment in PHEIs ranges from 17.9% to 28.2 % across the five years and the percentage of female enrolment rate is relatively higher in PHEIs compared to Public HEIs, which suggests that the PHEIs are contributing to the improvement of access in general and female participation in higher education in particular. Analysis of data on graduates (in all program levels) of both public and private HEIs also indicate that the share of graduates from PHEIs ranges from 16% to 41% across the five years, which again suggests that the PHEIs are contributing to the improvement of the trained human resource base of the country. Moreover, results of the interview data are in agreement with these findings. Almost all the interviewees drawn from public and private HEIs leaders, AEPHEIs representative, employers and parents believed that the PHEIs are playing their vital role in improving access to higher education and the human resources development of the country.

As regards PHEIs emphasis, the results in Table 3 indicate that majority of the student respondents agree that PHEIs give emphasis to maintain the relevance and quality of their education programs, whereas the agreement of the majority of the instructor respondents in this regard is moderate. In both cases, the difference in their ratings is significant. This finding is expected for the fact that students' views of relevance and quality may not necessarily match with the views of other stakeholders (in this case instructors). In most cases students choose their study program based on their perception of the relevance of the program in getting job after graduation, whereas the instructors could be more critical and pay attention to what goes on the actual teaching-learning process.

The current students were also asked to indicate the main reasons that forced them to join the PHEIs. Their responses indicate that lack of opportunity to join public HEIs (62.1%), better chance to enroll in their area of interest (61.8%) and better quality of education provided in PHEIs than the pubic ones (52.9%) are the main reasons for joining PHEIs. The interviews made with parents of the current students also revealed similar results. According to most of interviewed parents, lack of opportunity to join public HEIs is the main reason for sending their children to PHEIs. This shows that lack of opportunity to join public HEIs seems to be the primary reason for students to join PHEIs, which in turn suggests the assumption that students choose study programs based on their perceived relevance of the program is a secondary reason in this regard.

To corroborate the above findings, both current students and graduates were also asked about their level of satisfaction regarding the relevance of the education provided by their respective institution. Analysis of their responses indicated that the majority of both the current students and graduates are satisfied with the relevance of courses to improve knowledge and skill in their area of specialization, usefulness of the training program for their career development, and the effectiveness of PHEIs in producing graduates with marketable skills (see Table 5 below). The difference in their ratings is also highly significant across all items.

Table 5. Respondents' satisfaction with the relevance and quality of education offered by PHEIs

| Variables | Current students | | | Graduates | | |
|---|---|---|---|---|---|---|
| Satisfaction with: | High | Total | $\chi^2$ | High | Total | $\chi^2$ |
| Relevance of courses to improve knowledge in area of specialization | 252(81) | 312 | 318.3* | 51(73) | 70 | 51.8* |
| Relevance of courses to develop required skill in area of specialization | 254(82) | 309 | 335* | 54(76) | 71 | 59.4* |

| | | | | | | |
|---|---|---|---|---|---|---|
| Usefulness of program for career development | 251(81) | 310 | 321.8* | 51(71) | 72 | 47.3* |
| College's effectiveness in producing graduates with marketable skills | 211(68) | 310 | 172.9* | 53(75) | 71 | 17.3* |
| The extent to which the knowledge & skill acquired enable to pursue further education | | | | 56(88) | 64 | 133.6* |
| The current major area of study | 261 (85) | 307 | 294.2* | | | |

*$P< 0.01$. Note: Numbers in brackets are percentages.

The results in Tables 4 and 5 suggest that the PHEIs provide relevant education, as perceived by majority of the current students, instructors and graduates. Further analysis of documentary data was made to validate these findings.

It is assumed that both the education market and labor market determine the type of programs offered by PHEIs. In most cases, the for-profit PHEIs are market-friendly (Varghese 2006), and the relevance of their programs is conceived in terms of meeting market demands, i.e. employability of their graduates. In this regard, analysis of data on the types of study programs offered by the PHEIs across five years was made to see the relevance of their courses. The results are summarized in Table 6.

*Table 6. Types of study programs offered by PHEIs (2004/05-2008/09)\**

| Study Program | 2004/05 | 2005/06 | 2006/07 | 2007/08 | 2008/09 |
|---|---|---|---|---|---|
| Computer Science & Technology | 4775(14) | 1241(17) | 1898(24) | 2519(28) | 2134(8) |
| Natural & Computational Sciences | 3730(11) | 12(0) | 0 | 0 | 16(0) |
| Medicine & Health Sciences | 943(3) | 943(13) | 595(8) | 740(8) | 1573(6) |
| Agriculture & Life Sciences | 0 | 0 | 0 | 0 | 127(0) |
| Business & Economics | 23924(69) | 4231(59) | 4805(61) | 4726(53) | 23124(82) |
| Social Sciences & Humanities | 1351(4) | 757(11) | 585(7) | 907(10) | 1351(5) |
| **Total** | **34723** | **7184** | **7883** | **8892** | **28325** |

*SOURCE: Education Statistics Annual Abstracts (MoE, 2004/05-2008/09)

From the data in Table 6, it is noticeable that the PHEIs have been offering study programs that are dominantly in Business and Economics (Accounting & Finance, Management, Economics, Business Administration, Human Resource Management, Marketing, Procurement & Supply Management, Leadership & Development Studies, Secretarial Science & Office Management), followed by Computer Science and Technology (Business Information System, Information Technology, Computer Science and Engineering, Electronics and Computer Engineering, Electrical Engineering, Automotive Engineering & Vehicle Management, Construction Technology & Management, Architecture & Urban Planning). The issue here is whether these types of study programs are related to the labor market or not. Analysis of documentary evidences shows that the growth of the economy in the service sector has been relatively high for the last years. The development plan of the macro economy execution of the 2005-2010 indicated that there has been an average of 11% economic growth during this period, of which 14.6% average growth is in the service sector, 10% in industry and 8% in agriculture and related sectors (MoFED. 2010). This relatively high growth in the service sector of the economy implies more jobs and demand for trained labor force for employment, which suggests that training more people in the areas of Business & Economics, and Information & Communication Technology is highly probable to meet the employment demands in the service sector. The success of the PHEIs in this regard is determined by the employability of their graduates. To verify these assertions, analysis of documentary data on graduate employment was carried out by considering St. Mary's University College tracer study (SMUC, 2008).

The findings of this tracer study indicate that the graduates' employment rate, within six months after graduation, has been 44.2% on average for the period of seven years (2001-2007). The average employment rate goes up to 49% for the same period if the time elapsed until the first job obtained by a graduate was extended to nine months, and further up to 54.7% within a year. The employment rate ranges from 85.7% in 2001 to 47% in 2007, which shows a declining trend. With regard to field of study, the employment rate averaged to 41.6% for first degree level qualification, and varies between the lowest 22.2% in the case of management and the highest 58.8% for graduates of accounting department, whereas the employment rate for diploma level has been the highest (58.8%), within one year. The employment rate of SMUC graduates is 61.0% for the entire period since graduation. The private sector (49.5%), followed by government (39.0%), NGOs (10%) and others (2%) is the highest employer organization. These results show that SMUC has been producing relevant trained labor force for employment in the various private and government organizations.

The responses of the interviewees from the PHEIs leadership and parents substantiate the above results. The PHEIs leaders argue that their programs are relevant to the labor market and students' needs. The parents of PHEIs' graduates also share similar views that PHEIs provide relevant education to their children. Majority of the parent interviewees reported that the benefits of training provided by PHEIs outweigh the costs, although the tuition fee is not affordable to the low income group. In connection to this, the mother of a graduate from one of the sample PHEIs has the following to say:

> The benefit cannot be compared with the cost. We used to pay around 240 Birr per month for six semesters. Besides, we paid 170 Birr each month for three summer semesters. There were also other expenses. Covering all the costs was a challenge for us because I am a housewife and my husband earns little amount of money per month. After graduation, our daughter got a job and she is now earning a good monthly salary. So, we feel that those expenses are less than the benefits we are getting now" (P2, 15/03/2010).

From the above arguments, we can observe that the family's investment was worthwhile as their daughter got a job after graduation. Most of the parent interviewees have similar views, though they have concerns about getting jobs for their children immediately after graduation and the affordability of tuition fees.

However, the interviewees from HERQA have reflected their concerns regarding the relevance of education provided by PHEIs. As one of the interviewees from the Agency noted, most of the PHEIs focus on areas related to Business and Humanities, such as Accounting & Finance, Management, Economics, Marketing, Human Resource Management, Law, Education etc (O1, 30/03/2010). This raises a question as to why HERQA provided accreditation to PHEIs in the aforementioned study areas, if they are not deemed relevant to the market demand. It is known that the PHEIs open and run their programs based on the accreditation provided by HERQA. This shows that the responses of the interviewees from HERQA are contradictory to what HERQA has actually been doing in recognizing and accrediting the study programs of PHEIs and what is stated in Article 74 of the Higher Education Proclamation (No. 650/2009) regarding the rights of accredited institutions. The concern of the interviewees from employers is not as such on relevance of the study programs, rather they focus on the capacity of the PHEIs in equipping their graduates with the requisite knowledge, attitude and skills. In this connection, one of the interviewees noted that " PHEIs are good in terms of creating access to the needy students, but they don't have the required capacity to provide expected level of education" (E3, 07/03/2010).

The aforementioned results suggest that the PHEIs have been providing training programs that are related to the increasing demands for trained labor force of the service sector in both the private and government organizations. These findings are in agreement with the results of the institutional quality audit carried out in the five PHEIs, which affirms that most of the audited PHEIs have been offering employment oriented training programs (HERQA, 2009). These findings in turn corroborate the perceptions of current students, graduates and instructor respondents regarding the relevance of the study programs offered by PHEIs.

However, the relevance of the study programs is not sufficient; the quality of the study programs offered should also be an area of concern. The quality of the education provided by PHEIs is based on various factors, which includes among others: profile of their students, competence of instructors, availability and adequacy of learning resources (facilities, support services), appropriateness of their curricula and programs, performance of their graduates in the work place, etc. Further analysis of both quantitative and qualitative data was carried out on these and related issues. And the results are summarized in the subsequent tables.

The data in Table 7 indicate that the majority of the instructor respondents expressed their satisfaction concerning the commitment of their institution in ensuring professional competence of the academic staff, reviewing and improving quality of their curriculum and programs; ensuring the availability of adequate facilities; and providing quality education in general. The difference in the ratings of instructors is significant.

Table 7. Instructors' satisfaction with the commitment of their institution

| Variables | Satisfied | Total | $\chi^2$ |
|---|---|---|---|
| **Commitment of PHEIs in :** | | | |
| Reviewing and improving quality of curriculum & programs | 90 (68) | 133 | 71.5* |
| Ensuring the availability of adequate facilities | 93 (70) | 133 | 80.1* |
| Providing student support services | 88 (66) | 133 | 67.1* |
| Ensuring professional competence of academic staff | 103 (77) | 133 | 116.9* |
| Ensuring competence of graduates | 90 (67) | 134 | 76.6* |
| Providing quality education | 99 (74) | 134 | 99.2* |

*$P < 0.01$. Note: Numbers in brackets are percentages.

Current students and graduates were also asked about their perception regarding the adequacy of learning resources to provide quality education, and the results are summarized in Table 8 below. The findings indicate that the majority of the two groups of respondents expressed their satisfaction regarding the availability and adequacy of resources except one item, i.e. availability and adequacy of facilities, where the graduate respondents differ in their level of satisfaction, which could be due to changes in facilities of the institutions over time. The P-value, nonetheless, shows that the difference in their ratings is highly significant.

Overall, the findings in the above two tables suggest that the PHEIs have adequate learning resources, teaching staff and show their commitment to provide quality education, as perceived by the majority of the instructors, current students, and graduates.

*Table 8. Respondents' satisfaction with the availability and adequacy of resources*

| Variables | Current students | | | Graduates | | |
|---|---|---|---|---|---|---|
| | Satisfied | Total | $\chi^2$ | Satisfied | Total | $\chi^2$ |
| Adequacy of time allotted to complete training program | 225 (73) | 308 | 220.8* | 56 (78) | 72 | 72.4* |
| Availability and adequacy of support materials | 179 (77) | 232 | 68.4* | 48 (67) | 72 | 46.2* |
| Availability and adequacy of facilities | 187 (78) | 240 | 74.8* | 33 (46) | 72 | 29.9* |
| Availability of professionally competent instructors | 241 (79) | 307 | 283* | 57 (81) | 70 | 72.9* |

*$P< 0.01$. Note: Numbers in brackets are percentages

The students, graduates and instructors were also asked about their perception regarding the extent to which the PHEIs maintain the balance between their business motive (profit making) and stakeholders' (students, parents, employers, and government) needs. The results are summarized in Table 9 below.

Table 9. Respondents' ratings on the balance between business motive and stakeholders' expectations

| PHEIs give more emphasis to: | Students | | | Graduates | | | Instructors | | |
|---|---|---|---|---|---|---|---|---|---|
| | Agree | Total | $X^2$ | Agree | Total | $\chi^2$ | Agree | Total | $\chi^2$ |
| Their business motive | 199(66) | 303 | 145* | 25(39) | 64 | 20.7* | 104(95) | 109 | 89.9* |
| Maintain the balance between business motive & stakeholders' needs | 150(50) | 301 | 42.9* | | | | 56(42) | 132 | 16.5* |

*P< 0.01. Note: Numbers in brackets are percentages.

As can be observed from the data in Table 9, the majority of the current students and instructor respondents agreed with the assertion that PHEIs give more emphasis to their business motive (making profit), and the proportion of the two groups of respondents who contended that PHEIs emphasize maintaining the balance between their business motive and stakeholders' needs is relatively low. However, the majority of the graduates disagreed with this assertion. It is apparent that both students and instructors perceive the balance between business motive and meeting stakeholders' expectation from the angle of how the training programs are provided and managed, whereas the graduates perceive the issue from the perspective of their employability in the job market. This suggests that from the perspectives of the two groups of respondents, the two contradictory views may be considered possible responses, which needs to be validated further using qualitative data analysis.

The overall findings of the quantitative data analysis presented in the preceding Tables (Tables 7 to 9) show that the majority of the respondents (current students, instructors and graduates) have positive attitude regarding quality of the education provided by PHEIs in terms of reviewing and improving quality of curriculum and programs, and ensuring the availability of adequate learning resources (facilities; teaching personnel, student support services). The findings of respondents regarding the balance between the PHEIs business motive and meeting stakeholders' expectations are mixed, where the majority of the instructors and students reported that the PHEIs focus on their business motive, which is not the case with graduate respondents.

Further analyses of documentary and interview data were conducted to validate the perceptions of the respondents regarding quality of education in the PHEIs. Analysis of documentary data begins with the qualification mix of teaching personnel in PHEIs based on the education statistics annual abstracts of the

MoE, followed by analysis of the institutional quality audit reports of HERQA and then results of the interview data collected from sample respondents.

Analysis of the 2010/11 education statistics annual abstract of the MoE indicates that there are a total of 1493 full time Ethiopian academic staff across all PHEIs with a qualification mix of 53 (3.5%) Diploma, 591 (39.6%) Bachelor degree, 186 (12.5%) MD/MDV degree, 583 (39%) Masters degree, 69 (4.6%) Doctorate degree, and 11 (0.7%) others. Analysis of the qualification mix of full time Ethiopian academic staff was also carried out for some PHEIs based on the available current data. As can be seen from Table 10 below, the staff qualification mix of the PHEIs is dominated by Masters degree holders, except **Mekane Yesus Management & Leadership College and Africa Beza University College, which have more MD/MDV and Bachelor degree holders respectively.**

Table 10. *Qualification mix of full time Ethiopian academic staff for some PHEIs (2010/11)\**

| No. | Institutions | Diploma | Bachelor | MD/MDV | Masters | PhD | others | Total |
|---|---|---|---|---|---|---|---|---|
| 1 | Admas University College | 0 | 6 (7) | 0 | 70 (86) | 5 (6) | 0 | 81 |
| 2 | St. Mary's University College | 0 | 28 (29) | 0 | 61 (62) | 9 (9) | 0 | 98 |
| 3 | Unity University | 0 | 23 (28) | 0 | 42 (52) | 16(20) | 0 | 81 |
| 4 | Mekane Yesus Mgmt & Lead. College | 0 | 3 (21) | 9 (64) | 0 | 2 (14) | 0 | 14 |
| 5 | Africa Beza University College | 0) | 16 (55) | 12 (41) | 0 | 1 (3) | 0 | 29 |
| 6 | Mekelle Institute of Technology | 5 (11) | 19 (43) | 0 | 19 (43) | 1(2) | 0 | 44 |
| 7 | Sheba University College | 0 | 10 (14) | 1 (1) | 58 (79) | 4(5) | 0 | 73 |
|  | Total | 5 (1) | 105 (25) | 22 (5) | 250 (60) | 38 (9) | 0 | 420 |

\*SOURCE: Education Statistics Annual Abstract (MoE, 2010/11).

Note: Numbers in brackets are percentages.

These results suggest that the qualification mix of the teaching staff across all PHEIs and the sample ones does not coincide with the standard set by MoE, which demands staff qualification mix of 30% Doctorate degree, 50% Masters Degree and 20% Bachelor degree holders. This finding is not in parallel with the perceptions of instructors, students and graduates depicted in Tables 7 & 8 which indicated that the PHEIs have adequate and professionally competent teaching staff. The findings of the institutional quality audit carried out by HERQA on five PHEIs (Admas, City, Royal, and St. Mary's University Colleges; and Unity University) also corroborate the finding that the qualification mix of the academic staff falls short of that specified by MoE (HERQA 2009). These results suggest that the PHEIs have limitations in ensuring the required qualification mix of their teaching personnel, which is considered as one of the important components that influence quality of education.

Results of analysis of the institutional quality audit reports for the five PHEIs also disclosed that the institutions have some good practices in terms of establishing structures, committees and set of procedures for curriculum development and approval; introducing quality assurance structures; the efforts being made to conduct tracer studies of their graduates and introducing digital library services in some of the audited PHEIs (e.g. Royal and St. Mary's University Colleges). All the five PHEIs audited by HERQA (St. Mary's University College being the pioneer) have established quality assurance office/unit, except City University College, which is considered as an indication of the institutions' commitment for quality education.

However, lack of a planned program review, new curriculum approval and comprehensive documentation and decision-making criteria; absence of student-centred approaches; written policy on teaching, learning and assessment; and a comprehensive policy on quality assurance/ a well established and fully functional quality assurance system; shortage of library resources such as academic journals; low level of the use of audio visual resources; inadequacy of ICT services; lack of appropriate academic support (e.g. tutorials) and guidance & counseling services to needy students; lack of continuous consultations with stakeholders and systematic procedures to collect and disseminate information on graduate employment, employer satisfaction are found to be the major limitations of the five audited PHEIs (HERQA 2009). This suggests that the PHEIs have limitations in ensuring the conditions necessary to provide quality education.

The results of interview data analysis further indicate mixed views concerning quality of the training programs provided by PHEIs. As an interviewee from HERQA put it, 'there are problems in providing quality education both at the public and private higher education institutions. Some of them try to use HERQA's feedback to improve their programs; some of them try to be defensive.' (O1, 30/03/2010). Interviewees of the public HEIs also reported that most of the PHEIs have problems concerning the provision of quality education and their graduates don't have the requisite knowledge, attitude and skills. The interviewees from employers share similar views, in which majority of them reported that quality of the education provided by PHEIs is below their expectation. As one of the interviewees noted, "PHEIs don't have the required capacity to provide quality education; most of them do not have adequate library, laboratory, manpower and their own premises" (E3, 07/03/2010).

With regard to PHEIs' emphasis to maintain the balance between their business motives and meeting stakeholders' needs, the interview data revealed two divergent views. The first one refers to those PHEIs owned by investors whose main interest is profit-making. These types of institutions could predominantly focus on the business motive or the financial return of their investment (PIL2, 08/03/2010). One of the interviewees from public HEIs leaders also remarked that "There are PHEIs, which run their programs with unqualified instructors, have poor assessment and grading system and don't have tutorial program/support services for students who are weak in their performance" (PUL 3, 18/03/2010). Another interviewee from the sample public universities added that

> I know PHEIs which admit students to whichever department they like regardless of their academic background, duplicate curricula and programs of other HEIs and don't ensure student engagement, which compromise quality of the instructional process (PUL 6, 20/03/2010).

An interviewee from employers further added that "...most of the PHEIs do not satisfy the demands of the government as well as the community; they are very much more concerned about profit making than the provision of quality education" (E7, 07/03/ 2010). The views of employers corroborates with representative of AEPHEIs, in which the interviewee reported that it is difficult to put the level of satisfaction with regard to the current performance of PHEIs in terms of addressing stakeholders' expectations, i.e. employers and the government.

These findings unveil the fact that less emphasis given to quality education in PHEIs. There are also very serious issues regarding the trustworthiness of credentials and diplomas issued by PHEIs. In this connection, one of the interviewees from public HEIs (as an employer) reported the following

> It is observed that some students deal with some PHEIs to get their diplomas and degrees easily and quickly. Recently when we asked our employees to compete for vacant places created as a result of the BPR, there were some who submitted diplomas and degrees. But when we contacted the institutions, we found out that some of them have not been enrolled in those institutions at all. To address this kind of gap and until a

system of giving employment tests is developed, the measure taken by the government is proper (PUL 4, 10/03/2010).

Though there are no additional evidences on what happened with those institutions that issued false diplomas, the claim of the interviewee indicates the presence of some non-credible institutions that compromise quality education through selling fake diplomas and degrees. In this connection, Article 81 of the Higher Education Proclamation (No.650/2009) stated that the accreditation of any PHEI may be revoked 'where the institution fails… to satisfy the required standards or for contravening the provisions of the proclamation (p,5036).' There are, however, no officially documented evidences by HERQA or MoE regarding the measures taken against those PHEIs for violating the requirements of the proclamation and committing unethical behaviors.

The second view refers to those PHEIs established and owned by a group of professionals or non-profit organizations whose main interest is not only business but also service to society. Consistent with this view, interviewees from PHEIs leaders argue that they balance their business motives and meeting stakeholders' needs. One of the interviewed leaders of PHEIs asserted that

> Our main focus is whether students have got what they should for the money they paid. So we think that this institution is primarily educational institution and then business institution. Our business motive focuses on a long-term interest. This can simply be demonstrated by the income we collect from the students will be invested on enhancing students' learning process. The profit is not that much attractive for the institution as there are a lot of expenses. The system being practiced from the senate to the department council has been based on those type of organizations run through non-business elements (PIL1, 25/03/2010).

Supporting this argument, another interviewee noted the following:

> The college and its owners are very much concerned about quality education. Even though it is a business firm, the college is not primarily interested in gaining excessive profit; it rather focuses on keeping its reputation by providing standard and quality education with a fair financial gain. Thus, it tries to equilibrate the interests of the stakeholders. This can be demonstrated by the quality of instructors we hire and also the attractive salary we pay them which is the highest compared to the nearby HEIs. We also fulfill all the necessary educational equipment and materials with out incurring additional cost on our customers. We believe our business motive and stakeholders' expectations are balanced (PIL2, 08/03/2010).

From the above arguments, we can presume that all the PHEIs are not the same in properly executing their mandate. On the one hand, there are some PHEIs that predominantly focus on profit making and irresponsibly compromise stakeholders' needs in terms of quality of their services. On the other hand, there are PHEIs that give emphasis to addressing stakeholders' needs vis-à-vis their business motive.

In general, the findings in this section suggest that PHEIs are playing important role in creating access to those students who could not join public HEIs and improving the human resources development needs of the country by producing trained labor force that addresses the needs of the labor market. Nonetheless, most of the PHEIs have major limitations in ensuring the necessary conditions required to improve quality of their educational provisions, and thereby meeting their stakeholders' (employers) expectations, which needs due attention by PHEIs as well as other concerned stakeholders.

## 4.3 Government regulatory framework related to PHEIs

The regulatory framework is considered as a context in which public and private HEIs operate. Government regulatory framework embraces all aspects of the HEIs' relationship with government that ranges from the decision and approval of programs to regular monitoring and ensuring of policy implementation. In the Ethiopian context, there is no separate law or proclamation for PHEIs. It is the 2003 Higher Education Proclamation (351/2003), which was revised in 2009 (No. 650/2009), that serves as a basic legal framework for both public and private HEIs.

According to the Proclamation, PHEIs are subject to accreditation by HERQA, whereas accreditation is not a requirement for public HEIs. Article 74 of the Proclamation states that 'any person who desires to establish, upgrade or modify a private institution shall be required to secure an accreditation from the Ministry, and any institution which has received accreditation and offers accredited programs shall have the right to issue valid qualifications of higher education to its graduates' (p, 5031). This suggests that the PHEIs can directly get accreditation when the Agency ensures that the institutions satisfy the requirements set by the proclamation. This implies that accreditation for PHEIs is mandatory, rather than voluntary.

With regard to government subsidy for PHEIs, Article 86 of the Proclamation stipulated that 'the government may give budget subsidy or capacity building support to non-profit making PHEIs that strive to strengthen the developmental efforts of the country by preparing particularly good quality professionals' (p, 5024). Such government subsidy is based on certain preconditions in terms of undergraduate and graduate students' enrollment; number of full time academic staff employed, quality of education, past achievements of the institution in teaching & research, and the institutions' investment in facility development.

This indicates that government funding to PHEIs is not mandatory. Students' admission policy is also not the same for public and private HEIs, i.e. PHEIs admit those students who could not get the chance to join public HEIs.

It is apparent that both public HEIs and PHEIs are not equally treated in terms of accreditation, student admission policy and government funding, though they are required to operate under the same proclamation. Those public HEIs funded by the government are not subject to accreditation. On the contrary, those PHEIs which do not receive government funding are required for accreditation. At this point we can say that the rule of the game at policy level is not the same for private and public HEIs. Analysis of the quantitative data also revealed the following result (see Table 11).

Table 11. Instructors' opinion about regulatory frameworks related to PHEIs

| Variables | Agree | Total | $\chi^2$ |
|---|---|---|---|
| **Government regulatory frameworks (policy and laws):** | | | |
| Equally serve both public and private HEIs | 52 (39) | 132 | 46.409* |
| Encourage establishment of PHEIs | 74 (56) | 133 | 10.932* |
| Encourage students to join PHEIs | 56 (42) | 133 | 38.992* |
| Encourage parents to send their children to PHEIs | 59 (45) | 132 | 30.045* |
| Favor public HEIs | 92 (70) | 132 | 78.545* |
| Lack proper implementation concerning PHEIs | 84 (65) | 130 | 57.246* |

\* $P < 0.05$ Note: Numbers in brackets are percentages

As shown in Table 11, the majority of the instructor respondents agreed with the idea that government's regulatory framework favors public HEIs, lacks proper implementation concerning PHEIs, and encourages the establishment of PHEIs. On the other hand, a considerable portion of the respondents disagreed with the idea that the regulatory framework equally serves both public and private HEIs, encourages students to join PHEIs, and encourages parents to send their children to PHEIs. The results of the chi-square tests also revealed that there are statistically significant differences in the ratings of instructors across all items.

This suggests that the perception of instructors concerning the government regulatory framework is in agreement with the assertion that the rule of the game is not the same for both public and private HEIs. The responses of PHEIs leaders also revealed the following key issues concerning regulatory policy and laws:

1. The current Education and Training Policy or the Higher Education Proclamation by itself is not a serious problem for PHEIs.
2. The major problem is lack of stability and proper implementation of the policy and proclamation, i.e. problem of translating the regulatory policy and laws into action.
3. Differential treatment of PHEIs from public HEIs in terms of accreditation, student placement, etc. is also a hindrance to the smooth operation of PHEIs.

The following sample responses of the interviewees may help to illustrate the current issues concerning government regulatory framework related to PHEIs. As the interviewees noted, what the government needs or expects from PHEIs is clearly indicated in the new higher education proclamation, which abandoned the pre-accreditation requirements. As one of the interviewees put it, "The policy is conducive; it does not create unnecessary pressure and it allows PHEIs to do their job independently. PHEIs benefit a lot as long as they do not violate the proclamation and follow the regulations and directives" (PIL7, 11/03/ 2010). In the same vein, another interviewee added that:

> There is no fundamental difference between public institutions and ours regarding policy and related issues. In general, we want to take advantage of the policies and guidelines to benefit more from them; we do not see them as hindrances as they do not limit our height/success (PIL10, 04/03/2010).

The arguments presented so far indicate that the policy by itself is not a serious problem to start and run PHEIs. However, interviewees from both private and public HEIs articulated problems related to lack of stability and coherence and differential treatment in policy implementation. Regarding problems of implementation, one of the interviewees described the current situation as follows

> The major problem is that when we want to proceed as per the law, we come across with a number of irrelevant circulars, which totally distract the programs of the PHEIs. Our movement will be based on the will of assigned individuals who do not have enough knowledge/understanding of the matters. There are some cases by which we become disabled to proceed while the proclamation supports us. For example, on teacher education program, there came a circular, out of the blue, which declared that those who came from private institutions cannot be employed in public sectors. The other is about TVET programs, where we were forbidden not to offer our programs through distance education (PIL1, 25/03/2010).

Almost all the interviewees including leaders of public HEIs pointed out problems abounded with the proper implementation of the government's regulatory framework. There are also problems in terms of treating the public and private HEIs on an equal basis while implementing regulatory policy and laws. That is, implementation of the policy and laws is more stringent for PHEIs than the public ones. In line with this, one of the interviewees from PHEIs leaders noted the following:

> We don't have problem with the proclamation or policy. But, there are implementation problems/discriminatory practices such as HERQA's quality audit which is more stringent on PHEIs than in public HEIs, instructors as well as graduates of PHEIs do not have the opportunity to join public universities for further education, unfair student placement (PHEIs admit only those students who couldn't get the chance to join public HEIs), etc. (PIL 11, 04/03/2010).

Supporting the above argument, one of the public HEIs' leaders reflected as follows

> I don't think that the government regulatory laws and policy directives equally serve both the public and private HEIs. More focus is given to public HEIs. There is differential treatment, e.g. requirement of staff profile/qualification mix is not the same for both. There is a tendency to be strict on PHEIs (PUL3, 06/03/2010).

Moreover, there are inconsistencies and frequent changes in policy implementation through suddenly released circulars. As reported by the majority of the respondents from PHEIs leaders, the unexpected and frequent changes in TVET and teacher education programs are seriously affecting the operation of many PHEIs in terms of huge financial and investment crises. For example, as indicated in the Ethio Channel Newsletter published on Wednesday November 06, 2010, 50 PHEIs operating in the Addis Ababa City Administration have recently received warnings from the Regional TVET Agency in running their programs, out of which 5 of them are totally closed, 7 are partially closed and 38 are under warning (p,20). Similarly, 48 PHEIs that were operating in the Southern region of the country with an annual intake of 35,000 students have also been instructed by the respective government agencies to stop registering new entrants for the new academic year (Reporter Newsletter, August 04, 2010, 4). The main reasons cited for taking such measures on PHEIs in both cases are provision of poor quality education and violating government laws and regulations. It is apparent that such measures have negative effects on PHEIs in terms of financial loss and their credibility to their stakeholders, mainly students and parents.

The interviewees also pointed out that there are no transition periods and exit strategies when policy instruments are suddenly changed. The recent circular/directive concerning educational quality and relevance, which is issued by the Ministry of Education (dated 20/12/2002 E.C.; Ref. No. 1/1-14058/2329/...) is a good example in this regard.

The new directive instructs both public and private HEIs to implement policy changes in several areas related to academic programs. The policy shift that specifically concerns PHEIs includes:

- Discontinuation of new/fresh students admission in undergraduate and post graduate distance education programs. This also applies to public HEIs,
- Suspending the provision of new accreditation or renewals to PHEIs for new regular program or expanding enrolment capacity or opening new branches for the existing ones, until a new quality assurance mechanism is devised. Renewal of accreditation is possible based on evidences of relevance and quality of the training programs approved by HERQA.
- Banning the renewal of accreditation for regular undergraduate and post graduate programs in the fields of law and teacher education. PHEIs are no longer allowed to offer training programmes in these fields. Training programs in these areas of study are to be offered in public HEIs only.
- Admitting students to regular programs based on the minimum entry requirements set by the Ministry of Education.

The issuance of the new directive is surprising to many and it has raised a lot of reactions on the part of PHEIs leaders/owners and EPHEIs Association. As indicated in the Fortune Newspaper published on Sunday August 29, 2010; the new directive is hard to grasp by a lot of people at the helm of PHEIs and most of them lamented that "Instead of resorting to such drastic measures to ensure quality, working on the criteria for quality standards should have been a priority" (p,8). The PHEIs leaders feel that the new directive will have an adverse effect on the private provision of higher education in the country. In this Newspaper, one of the PHEIs leaders argued that "The current inability of the government to enforce the quality standards already set should not lead to these kinds of measures...." (p,8).

The discussions in the preceding paragraphs raise questions as to why and what ground did the Ministry issue the circulars and take measures at this time. What is the reason for prohibiting PHEIs to run training in the areas of law and teacher education? Interviews on these and related issues were conducted with high level official of the Ministry of Education. From the interview, it was learnt that since June 2006 the Ministry has been engaged in implementing five major reform agendas in public HEIs including BPR, curricular change, teacher development, the undergraduate professional and program mix, and changing the higher education proclamation. In this regard, the assumption of the Ministry was that the PHEIs apply what is stated in the proclamation and realize the government reforms that took place in public HEIs. This is, however, not the case with the PHEIs. As the Ministry official put it:

> The new HE proclamation has clearly stipulated the role of PHEIs in its preamble, but the institutions have remained passive in translating the requirements of the proclamation into action. Besides, the Ministry has held a meeting with private providers to create common understanding on pertinent issues contained in the proclamation. The PHEIs, however, focus on procedures rather than on the content of the proclamation. It is about two years since the promulgation of the new HE proclamation, which is a reasonably adequate lead-time to make necessary adjustments. Hence, PHEIs were supposed to react proactively and seriously follow up the changes being introduced in public HEIs because these changes have their bearing on the operation of PHEIs. So, their complaint is not justifiable (O2, 28/09/2010).

With regard to the restrictions imposed on teacher education and law fields of study, the Ministry official further noted the following as the main reason:

> The fields of studies in teacher education and law are by their nature crucial and all encompassing that determine the fate of the nation in many aspects. Offering quality and effective training in these fields of study is difficult to realize in PHEIs and through distance mode. Thus, the government can not afford to allow PHEIs offer such study programs. These training programs can only be offered in public HEIs, where the government has direct intervention in terms of funding and administration (O2, 28/09/2010).

From the above discussions, it is clear that the PHEIs in our country are in a state of turmoil due to lack of stable, consistent, coherent and proper implementation of the government's regulatory framework, which includes policy directives, laws and regulations, though the decisions and actions taken are considered as timely and legitimate by higher officials of the MoE. Such trends would obviously have a negative impact on the smooth operation of the private sector in the country as well as its beneficiaries ---students and employees of PHEIs as well as parents. There is no disagreement between and among the respondents from leaders of both public and private HEIs as well as from officials of the Ministry regarding the need for the implementation of the government's regulatory laws and policy directives. The main issues observed as points of debate and disagreement are related to the lack of consistency/stability, uniformity and transition period in the implementation of the government's regulatory framework.

From the government side, there is no doubt that the Ministry has the responsibility to make sure that the society gets quality service from both public and private higher education institutions. The PHEIs should also be accountable to their stakeholders in providing relevant and quality educational services. This requires developing and implementing a robust regulatory framework which enables to ensure that all parts of the higher education sector are monitored and regulated to similar standards including accreditation. It is known that the government has setup HERQA with the mandate to monitor and regulate the relevance and quality of education provided by all HEIs in the country. Accordingly, the PHEIs have been operating based on the recognition and accreditation provided by HERQA. Despite this fact, the Ministry has recently issued a circular that requires PHEIs to abandon their programs in distance education as well as in the fields of Law and Teacher Education. However, the Agency was supposed to take timely measures to correct ill-practices observed in the operation of PHEIs and thereby ensure the relevance and quality of educational provision. This was, however, not the case with HERQA. In this regard, the recently issued circular and frequent changes in policy directives that are applicable across all PHEIs indicate the failure of the Agency to distinguish those credible PHEIs from the ones with ill-practices, and take corrective measures in advance before problems get worse. The official from the Ministry also admitted that HERQA does not have the competence and implementation capacity to closely follow-up and ensure quality of educational services in all HEIs and thereby realize its mandate stipulated in the Proclamation.

Further analysis of recently issued government documents indicated that a task force composed of members from HERQA, REBs, TVET agencies, and professionals from MoE was formed to evaluate the performance of 75 PHEIs operating across all regions based on the following nine evaluation criteria: (a)governance system of PHEIs, (b) academic programs and organization, (c) curriculum, (d) teachers, (e) students' learning assessment system, (f) students admission, registration, record keeping and support services, (g) conduciveness of learning environment and infrastructure, (h) internal quality assurance system, (i) research budget administration and outputs.

Based on the results of the evaluation conducted in 2011, out of the 75 PHEIs, 57 were identified as capable to run their training programs, 13 were classified as PHEIs that fulfil the minimum standard, and 5 were unable to fulfil the minimum standard and thus decided to terminate their training programs (HERQA, 2011).

Moreover, evaluation of the distance education programs run by both PHEIs and public university and cross-border education run by some PHEIs has been conducted based on the aforementioned evaluation criteria and competence based tests administered to students of PHEIs on selected programs. Accordingly, six private and six public HEIs were classified as capable to continue their training in undergraduate programs; the other three public and nine private HEIs were identified as incapable to fulfil the minimum standard, but allowed to continue their existing training programs till final decision is made on the basis of further evaluation on their programs. Apart from this, five PHEIs were able to get permission to continue their cross-border education since they fulfil the minimum standard (Addis Zemen News letter, Hidar 28, 2004 E.C.).

The evaluation results discussed above show that significant number of both private and public HEIs have been running their programs without fulfilling the required training standards. The results also suggest that the problem of low quality education is related to both private and public providers of higher education. Such evaluation may be considered as a good start in terms of regulating the quality and relevance education provided by higher education institutions of the country. However, this would have been better, if the Ministry/HERQA had undertaken such evaluation and corrective measures on an on-going, timely and comprehensive fashion.

The overall findings in this section unveil that the content of the recently issued circular and policy directives as well as the evaluation measures dwell on provision of poor quality education in PHEIs. Nevertheless, this poses a fundamental question on whether the PHEIs are inferior to public HEIs in quality of their study programs as demonstrated by the evaluation results. A closer examination of the institutional quality audit reports published by HERQA also indicates that there is a serious concern of quality in both public and private HEIs. In this connection, the Ministry has been expressing its concerns through conferences and media regarding quality of the education provided by public HEIs. This suggests that the issue of quality refers not only to PHEIs as there are also concerns of poor quality education in both the old and newly emerging public HEIs. Issuing circulars and policy directives that are applicable only to all PHEIs is, therefore, not convincing and justifiable.

## 4.4 Public-private partnerships

The public higher education sector today accounts for a considerable share of programs and student enrolment in the higher education system of the country. The contribution of the private higher education sector in improving access to higher education has increased over the past years. It is believed that if the contribution of the private higher education sector is recognized in the strategic development of the higher education sector through improving access, then a coordinated partnership of the public and private higher education institutions is crucial. Partnership refers to a cooperative venture between the public and private sectors to best meet clearly defined public needs, which include collaboration in program/curriculum design and improvement, maintaining standards in student intake and training, resources sharing and staff exchange, and in policy making and improvement. According to Haileleul (2007), the key partnership areas between public and private HEIs may include: joint employment of academic staff, sharing resources, joint research and publications, sharing curriculum, joint curriculum development, organizing joint conferences, staff exchange and shadowing, joint quality assurance undertakings, establishing a nationwide forum for public -private partnership.

At macro level, the partnership between public and private HEIs is not well articulated. Article 58 of the Proclamation states that 'public HEIs may establish a forum with appropriate name, to coordinate efforts, harmonize academic standards and approaches, share experience, and to advise the Ministry on national and international strategic issues, trends and conditions of higher education" (p, 5021), whereas the partnership between public and private HEIs is not properly articulated. As indicated in Sub- Article 9 under Article 58 of the Proclamation, 'there may be as necessary consultative partnerships between the forum of public HEIs and any legally established associations of PHEIs' (p, 5022). This suggests that the type and nature of the partnership between the public and private HEIs is not given due attention, and the consultative partnership highlighted in the proclamation is not strong enough to boost realistic partnership between the two sectors and the government. In this connection, sample respondents were asked about their views regarding the degree of partnership between the public and private HEIs. Results of the quantitative and qualitative data analyses are presented below.

Table 12. *Respondents' ratings on the status of public-private partnerships*

| Variables | Current students | | | Instructors | | |
|---|---|---|---|---|---|---|
| | Yes | Total | $\chi^2$ | Yes | Total | $\chi^2$ |
| Public-private partnership is based on competition | 174(78) | 223 | 70.1* | 61(48) | 127 | 24.4* |
| There is healthy relationship between PHEIs and government | 143(70) | 203 | 33.9* | 26(20) | 132 | 12.7* |

*$P< 0.01$, **$P< 0.05$. Note: Numbers in brackets are percentages

According to the data in Table 12, the majority of the students reported that the public-private partnership is based on competition between public and private HEIs and there is a healthy relationship between PHEIs and government, whereas. The same was not found to be case for instructors. That is the majority of the instructors indicated that the public-private partnership is not based on competition and the relationship of PHEIs with the government is not healthy. These responses of the students are not in agreement with the findings in section 4.3, i.e. the rule of the game is not equal for public and private HEIs. The public and private HEIs, for example, do not compete for resources and students' admission, and all public HEIs depend on government funding whereas PHEIs depend on tuition fees.

The interviews with leaders of public HEIs also show that there is no formally established partnership between their institution and the nearby private HEIs. As one of the interviewees noted, there is moonlighting by instructors of both public and private HEIs, which is not grounded in officially agreed staff exchange schemes between the two sectors (PUL3, 11/03/2010). There are also instances where public HEIs utilize teaching staff from PHEIs (e.g. Bahirdar University from GAMBY College of Medical Sciences; Haramaya University from Horn College). In addition to this, PHEIs seem to play complimentarity roles in terms of access because they accommodate those students who could not get places in public HEIs. With regard to their relation with the government, most leaders of PHEIs believe that they have good relationship with the government in many areas except the frequently observed problems of policy implementation, including accreditation.

The findings in this section in general suggest that the pubic- private partnership is not well developed in terms of collaborative venture between the public and private HEIs to address societal needs. The relationship between the PHEIs and government is also not to the expected level in terms of enhancing the smooth functioning of the private sector compared to the public ones. What is highlighted in the Proclamation regarding consultative partnership is not strong enough and detailed to boost realistic partnership between public and private HEIs.

## 4.5. Employers' Satisfaction with the Performance of Graduates from PHEIs

One of the basic questions of this study was to explore employers' satisfaction with the performance of graduates from PHEIs. In this regard, employers were asked to express their level of satisfaction. The responses of employers are mixed regarding this issue. One group of respondents expressed their satisfaction and they argue that graduates of PHEIs and public HEIs are more or less comparable in terms of their performance.

An interviewee from one of the branches of the Ethiopian Telecommunications Corporation with 10% of its total employees (115) are graduates of PHEIs, noted the following:

> We are more or less satisfied with the performance of PHEIs graduates although the performance varies from individual to individual based on their ability and effort. Each HEI has its own strengths and weaknesses. There are even graduates from PHEIs, who perform better than that of the public ones. The graduates of PHEIs may have some deficiency in their professional competence. This problem is also manifested in the graduates of public HEIs (E10, 15/02/2010).

The interviewee from one of the branch offices of the Ethiopian Insurance Corporation with 16% of the total employees (49) are graduates of PHEIs, noted that the there are good and bad performers from public as well as PHEI graduates. Similarly, one of the owners of GAMBY Hospital, which has a total of 49 employees, out of which 41% are graduates of PHEIs, expressed his satisfaction with the performance of PHEIs' graduates. Other interviewees from Awash Bank and Asher General Hospital also share similar views.

The other group of respondents from employers expressed their dissatisfaction with the performance of PHEIs' graduates. The interviewees in this group reflected that graduates of public HEIs have better grasp of the required knowledge, skill, and attitude than that of the PHEIs. The data obtained from one of the branch offices of the Commercial Bank of Ethiopia revealed that 30% of its total employees (401) are graduates of PHEIs. One of the interviewees from this branch office remarked that

> PHEIs' graduates don't have the necessary knowledge, skill and ability. This is manifested when we hold interview with them and ask specific questions related to the actual work. Usually they fail to give proper

responses to the questions. They fail to express their ideas in English, put into practice what they have learnt; they don't know the basic principle of some courses such as Accounting, they are not change oriented and ready to face challenges. This indicates that there is problem in the quality of education provided in the PHEIs. (E1, 10/03/2010).

Another interviewee from the Ethiopian Electric Power Corporation branch office with 16% of its total employees (755) are PHEI graduates added that the graduates of PHEIs lack the necessary knowledge, skill and attitude to perform well in their assigned duties compared to graduates of public HEIs. Although the above findings suggest divergent views about the performance of PHEI graduates, most of the interviewed employers witnessed that the performance of PHEIs graduates is not necessarily inferior to the graduates of public HEIs.

In general, it is possible to presume that the satisfaction of employers concerning the performance of graduates from PHEIs depends very much on the demonstrable ability and effort of graduates in the actual work setting rather than the type of institutions they have graduated from.

### 4.6. Opportunities and Challenges of PHEIs

One of the focal areas of the study was identifying the opportunities and major challenges encountered in the operation of PHEIs. Accordingly, a brief discussion on these issues is presented hereunder.

*Opportunities*

The opportunities that encourage the development and operation of private higher education in Ethiopia, according to the PHEIs leaders and/or owners, are the higher education proclamation that allows the establishment of private higher education institutions, and the policy environment that emphasizes the expansion of higher education as well as technical and vocational education. Moreover, the bulge in secondary school enrolment and the consequent increasing demand for higher education; relevance of the courses and programs offered in PHEIs to the country's changing labor market demand; the introduction of cost sharing system in the public universities; the economic and social policies adopted by the government and the increasing need on the part of the private sector to invest in higher education; and the recently recorded growth per capita income, which expands the higher education consumption of the general public; can be considered as the opportunities that encourage the development of private higher education in the country (Nwuke, 2008).

However, the aforementioned opportunities are not up to the expectation of stakeholders, especially due to implementation problems, and not comparable with other neighboring African countries. For instance, in Kenya, private higher education institutions are considered as the main partners of the higher education strategic plan for improving access and easing an admissions crisis that public universities have been unable to resolve. Recently, the Kenyan government has announced that private higher education institutions will admit at least 25, 000 government sponsored students in the next two years (Nganga, 2010). This shows the government's commitment to encourage private higher education institutions to play their role in the expansion of higher education in the country. This, however, is not the case in Ethiopia. In the paragraphs that follow, the major challenges facing Ethiopian PHEIs are presented.

## *Challenges*

Sample respondents (instructors and students) were asked to identify the major challenges from a given list of possible factors that are assumed to negatively affect the operation of PHEIs. Accordingly, the majority of the students (63%) and all instructors reported that lack of government support is the major challenge facing PHEIs. The $\chi^2$ test for the differences in the ratings of both groups is significant at $P<0.01$. This result corroborates the findings in the preceding sections that there are limitations regarding government support in terms of embedding robust regulatory framework that equally serves both public and private HEIs; implementing market principles that encourage constructive competition within and between public and private HEIs through different incentive schemes; creating mechanisms that boost partnership between the government, public and private HEIs in maintaining and improving access, relevance and quality of higher education.

Further analysis of interview data secured from PHEIs leaders was conducted to substantiate the above findings. Most of the sample PHEIs leaders/owners observed that government support for PHEIs in terms of incentives and equal treatment with public HEIs is almost non-existent, though the higher education proclamation allows the opening and functioning of PHEIs in the country. As one of the interviewees argued, "there is poor administrative and technical support from local state representatives in opening and approving study programs due to lack of understanding and due to failure in translating what is stipulated in the Proclamation by the concerned government bodies; sudden/untimely decisions are made against the operation of PHEIs (such as circular that requires closure of programs in distance education) without considering the huge investment made on the institutions (e.g. Alpha and St. Mary's University Colleges). Due to to such challenges, owners of such PHEIs are forced to close some of their programs and change their strategies "(PIL6,

18/03/2010). The major findings regarding the challenges facing PHEIs in Ethiopia are further thematically summarized as follows.

## *The Market*

The findings in section 4.3 indicated that the rule of the game is not the same for public and private HEIs in terms of accreditation, student admission and government incentives. For example, the PHEIs have no equal chance with public HEIs to compete for incoming students. They have to enroll low achieving students who do not get the opportunity to join public HEIs. The market is not free for PHEIs to enroll best students. This suggests that it is a challenge for PHEIs to produce quality graduates by enrolling those students with lower entry requirements.

As one of the interviewees noted, "If there is no free flow of students, the PHEIs will always be in danger. The tuition fee is also dependent on the market or the students' ability to pay" (PIL1, 25/03/2010). This evidently affects the operation of PHEIs in ensuring the quantity and quality of their incoming students. On the contrary, the public HEIs are forced to enroll too many students irrespective of their resources and capacity in terms of space, accommodation and library facilities, academic staff etc. This indicates that the application of market principles is not a reality in the Ethiopian context. This is a challenge for PHEIs to smoothly operate and contribute towards the strategic development of the higher education sector.

## *Government Regulatory Policy and Laws*

The government's policy and laws by themselves may not be considered as a challenge. The Higher Education Proclamation allows the establishment of PHEIs and their co-existence with the public ones. The major challenge facing PHEIs is "the problem of properly translating the policies and laws into action. The implementation of regulatory policy and laws is more stringent on PHEIs than public HEIs. For example, whereas HEIs are subject to accreditation, the public ones are not" (PIL4, 15/03/2010). The PHEIs are recently facing challenges in running their programs due to the inconsistency and frequent changes of the existing laws. As one of the interviewees from PHEIs leaders noted, the frequently changing nature of laws and regulations, making decisions suddenly without justifiable reasons and reasonable transition period is becoming a major challenge for PHEIs (PIL3, 10/03/2010). The findings in section 4.3 also demonstrated that the government's regulatory system is not robust and dynamic to monitor and regulate the relevance and quality of the higher education system, identify malpractices and take timely corrective measures. The inconsistency in policy directives suggests that the government seems to maintain its relationship with PHEIs on an ad hoc basis with a tendency to fight fires as they arise rather than embedding and relying on a robust, comprehensive and dynamic regulatory system. The absence of such a reliable system evidently affects the smooth functioning of PHEIs.

## *Relevance and Quality*

The findings in section 4.2 demonstrated that the PHEIs have been contributing to improve access and producing trained labor force to the labor market. All programs offered by PHEIs are subject to accreditation and quality assurance requirements of HERQA. However, PHEIs enroll those students who could not get the opportunity to join public HEIs due to their low performance in national exams. It is a challenge for PHEIs to train such students with poor academic background and produce quality graduates. Getting/hiring highly qualified instructors is also frequently cited as one of the major problems which affect the provision of quality education in PHEIs. These and other input and process related issues have a negative impact on the outputs expected from PHEIs.

## 4.7. Discussion of the major findings

There is a growing concern regarding the smooth operation of the private higher education sector in Ethiopia. In this study, an attempt was made to explore how the PHEIs in Ethiopia are operating in terms of improving access to higher education; and relevance and quality of their study programs vis-à-vis the existing government regulatory framework. The findings of the analysis of quantitative and qualitative data revealed that the PHEIs are playing vital roles in creating access to those citizens who could not get opportunities to be enrolled in public HEIs despite the fact that the majority of the PHEIs are profit driven and focus on market-friendly training programs. In this respect, the PHEIs' role seems complimentary in improving access because a large share of student enrolment is still dominated by public HEIs. In Geiger's (1986) classification, the PHEIs in Ethiopia may be grouped under the peripheral type of private sector. This is similar with the findings of Varghese's (2006) research about the trends in other African countries such as Uganda, Tanzania, Ghana, etc, where the public sector dominates the higher education system. In Marginson's (2007) description, the dominance of the public sector over the private sector shows the enhancement of public goods relative to private goods in the provision of higher education.

With regard to relevance and quality of education, the results of the study unveiled that the education provided by PHEIs is relevant as perceived by the internal constituents of the institutions, which includes current students, graduates, instructors and PHEIs' leaders. Results of documentary analysis, such as the tracer study conducted by St. Mary's University College, HERQA's quality audit reports and the Education Statistics Annual Abstracts of the MoE, also concur with the perceptions of the sample respondents. However, analysis of employers' responses and documentary evidences show that the PHEIs have limitations in providing quality education that addresses the expectations of their stakeholders, although the students and instructors claimed that their respective institutions provide quality education. In this study, quality of education is conceptualized from the stakeholders' perspective as defined by Tam (2001). Hence, the responses of graduates and employers are considered as the ultimate evidences concerning quality of graduates since the training programs of PHEIs focus on marketable skills that address the demands of the labor market (employers).

The findings of this study further revealed that the main issue is not relevance of the training programs run by PHEIs, but quality of the education provided. However, the problems related to quality are not unique to PHEIs, as there are HEIs from both public and private sectors that fail to provide quality education to their stakeholders. As the findings disclosed, there are PHEIs, which predominantly focus on profit making regardless of the quality of their services and those which respond to stakeholders' needs vis-à-vis their business motive. Thus, it is possible to argue against the claim that all PHEIs compromise the relevance and quality of their programs, and produce poor quality graduates.

As argued by Dill (2005), the public interest is best served by regulatory policies and laws, which assure that the higher education system, regardless of the form of ownership (public or private), provides quality human capital. In this regard, the government's regulatory frameworks are considered effective when they encourage and enable both public and private HEIs to produce quality graduates and services to the labor market. However, the findings in this study demonstrated that both public and private HEIs are not equally treated in terms of accreditation, student placement, government funding, etc. although they are required to operate under the same policy and proclamation. The application of the government's regulatory policy and laws are more stringent on PHEIs than the public ones, which suggests that the regulatory framework is in favor of public HEIs. In Zumeta's (1997) classification, the existing government regulatory framework is neither the market competition nor the central planning policy posture; rather the laissez-*faire* approach seems to prevail in the Ethiopian context.

As the findings indicated, although there are policy and labor market related opportunities that encourage the development of PHEIs in the country, they are not up to the expectation of stakeholders, and comparable with the opportunities in other African countries. It was also found out that PHEIs are facing a series of challenges in smoothly running their programs due to lack of comprehensive, robust, and reliable government regulatory framework. The existing regulatory policy and laws are inconsistent and unstable, and do not encourage the application of market principles and strategic partnership within and between public and private HEIs. The rule of the game is not the same for public and private HEIs in terms of constructive competition for incoming students and government incentives. However, as noted by Cheng (2009), the contribution of higher education to national development relies on developing credible alliances based on mutual trust and cooperation between the public and private providers of higher education. The findings in this study, however, revealed that the ideal conditions necessary for successful public-private partnership (suggested by Bjarnason et al. 2009) are not in place in the Ethiopian context. The consultative public-private partnership highlighted in the Higher Education Proclamation is not strong enough to boost mutual trust and cooperation in the strategic development of the higher education sector. As Haileleul (2007) pointed out, the absence of policy framework on partnership between public and private higher education institutions has reduced the relevance and quality of higher education in the country.

Moreover, it can be argued that in a situation where there is no robust and reliable regulatory framework and an autonomous agency, it is very difficult to ensure the contribution of PHEIs in improving access and quality of higher education in the country. The recently issued government circulars, which presuppose the provision of poor quality education in PHEIs, are not grounded on sound evidence. As Nwuke (2008) warned, quality of education is likely to deteriorate in the absence of strong and robust regulatory framework, and it is difficult to ensure relevance and quality of education through the application of rules and regulations that apply only to PHEIs in a context where the public provision of higher education is still dominant.

Overall, the findings of the study suggest that the overarching reason for the prevailing malpractices and chaos in the provision of quality education and the challenges facing PHEIs in smoothly running their programs is the absence of robust, comprehensive, and reliable government regulatory framework and, an autonomous implementing Agency.

## 5. Concluding Remarks and Recommendations

### 5.1 Concluding remarks

The major purpose of this study was to explore the current issues in PHEIs and uncover the impact of regulatory practices on the operation of PHEIs as well as identify the opportunities that encourage and the major challenges that hinder the smooth operation of PHEIs. To this end, data were collected from different sources and analyzed quantitatively and qualitatively so as to shed light on the current condition of PHEIs in the country. The following concluding remarks are derived from the major findings of the study.

- The PHEIs are playing their vital role in creating increased access to higher education for those citizens who could not get opportunities to be enrolled in public HEIs, though the majority of the PHEIs are profit driven and focus on market-friendly training programs. Despite their commendable role in this regard, they, however, seem to play complimentary role since a large share of student enrolment is still dominated by public HEIs. In this context, the PHEIs in Ethiopia may be categorized under the peripheral type of private providers of higher education.

- The main issues revolving around the operation of PHEIs are not as such on the relevance of their training programs but rather on quality of their educational provision. The problems related to quality, however, are not unique to PHEIs, as there are HEIs from both public and private sectors that fail to provide quality education and satisfy the expectations of their stakeholders. All public as well as private HEIs are not the same in the provision of quality education. There are PHEIs, which predominantly focus on profit making and those, which maintain the balance between their business motive and meeting the needs of their stakeholders, mainly employers. The claim that all PHEIs compromise the relevance and quality of their programs is, therefore, not well founded as demonstrated by the results of the recently conducted evaluations on both private and public HEIs.

- A partnership that boosts joint venture, mutual trust and cooperation among government, public and private HEIs is not well developed in the country. The consultative public-private partnership highlighted in the Higher Education Proclamation is not strong enough to enhance strategic partnership between and among public and private HEIs.

- The market principles that encourage constructive competition between public and private HEIs are not being properly implemented in the Ethiopian context. The rule of the game does not allow PHEIs to compete with public HEIs in terms of student placement and government incentives. This obviously affects the fate of private providers in the country.
- There is no separate proclamation for PHEIs, i.e. both public and private HEIs are required to operate under the same proclamation. However, both the public and private providers are not equally treated in terms of accreditation, student placement, staff development, and government funding. The government's regulatory policy and laws are found to be more stringent on PHEIs than the public ones, which implies the application of double standard in the higher education landscape. Such differential treatment has an adverse effect on the growth and contribution of PHEIs in the strategic development of the higher education sector. There is also lack of stability and consistency as well as frequent changes in the existing regulatory policy and laws. This is an indication for the absence of robust and comprehensive government regulatory framework and failure of the HERQA to periodically monitor and follow up the operation of both public and private HEIs up to the expected level.

In general, it is possible to presume that the overarching reason for the prevailing malpractices and chaos in the name of 'quality assurance' resides in the limitations of the government regulatory framework. And without embedding a robust and comprehensive regulatory system that encourages constructive competition and strategic partnership between and among those parties, which have stake and vested interest in the Ethiopian higher education system; ensuring the relevance and quality of higher education in the country would be difficult if not impossible.

## 5.2 Recommendations

Based on the aforementioned findings of the study and concluding remarks, the following policy implications/recommendations are forwarded so as to be considered by the PHEIs, AEPHEIs, as well as the Government/MoE/HERQA.

## a) PHEIs

It is believed that the responsibility of ensuring the relevance and quality of education that addresses the needs of stakeholders primarily relies on the institutions themselves. Accordingly, the PHEIs should:

- Make sure that they are operating in such away that their training programs are affordable and up to the standard in terms of meeting the increasing needs of the country for skilled labor force. It is also imperative for private institutions to gauge their contributions for national development. This requires, among others, ensuring that:
  - The infrastructure, learning resources and facilities are adequate to provide relevant and quality education, which requires from the institutions the mobilization of available resources and giving priority for availing such input variables,
  - The teaching staff is adequate and professionally competent to run programs to the expected standard. Thus, the institutions should design and implement their staff development plans in consultation with the Ministry of Education, other public HEIs as well as through creating linkages with similar overseas higher education providers,
  - An institutionalized culture of periodically reviewing the relevance and quality of the training programs is embedded, and
  - There is continuous improvement of programs/ curricula, teaching- learning process based on the feedback from need assessment, graduate tracer studies, institutional self-evaluation and external quality audit reports.
- Avoid duplication of study programs or curricula with public HEIs. In this regard, PHEIs should exploit the market needs by focusing on niches in their study programs.
- Respond proactively to policy changes and actively participate in translating and improving regulatory policy and laws.

## b) AEPHEIs

Associations or unions of private providers play important role in enabling PHEIs address the needs of their stakeholders in terms of providing relevant and quality services as well as protecting the rights of private providers. In the Ethiopian context, the PHEIs have their own association (AEPHEIs) with similar mission, though all PHEIs have not joined the Association. In order to play its critical role in improving the contribution of PHEIs in the country, the Association should:

- Build its capacity by increasing the number of member institutions and strengthening its linkages with similar overseas associations/ organizations,
- Actively participate in accreditation and quality audit activities and work closely with the government (MoE/HERQA), employers, public HEIs and similar professional organizations so as to improve the performance as well as sustain the fate of PHEIs,
- Serve as a forum for PHEIs to identify their limitations and continuously improve the relevance and quality of their training programs,
- Encourage those PHEIs which took the initiative to set up and implement quality assurance units/centers and give the necessary support for those which failed to embed quality assurance mechanisms,
- Support research endeavors on critical issues surrounding the operation of PHEIs in the country.

## c) Government/MoE/ HERQA.

The government has the mandate to assure that the higher education sector provides relevant and quality services to its immediate beneficiaries in particular and contributes to the overall development of the country. Hence, it should:

- Recognize and appreciate the contributions of PHEIs in the strategic development of the higher education sector in terms of increasing access and thereby improving the trained human resource base of the country;
  - Make sure that there is a robust and comprehensive regulatory framework and autonomous implementing agency that equally serves the public and private providers of higher education. Hence, like in other African countries such as Nigeria, South Africa, Ghana, etc.; HERQA should be autonomous and be given the mandate to accredit both public and private HEIs. HERQA, on its part, ought to build its capacity in such a way that it can accomplish its tasks specified in the proclamation, has its own policy which governs its

operation, and develop a culture of looking inward and periodically reviewing its weaknesses and strengths;

- Set reasonable quota for PHEIs (20-30%) of further education opportunities so as to build the professional capacity of the teaching staff, solve shortage of highly qualified staff, and thereby enable them meet the staff mix requirements set for accreditation;

- Adopt the Kenyan experience and revise the existing student placement policy so that eligible students are also placed in PHEIs with the necessary government support;

- Play its regulatory role in undertaking quality review professes on an on-going, timely and comprehensive way. Also, making the rule of the game equal to both providers of higher education and minimize discriminatory application of sanctions in the name of quality assurance; and

- Ensure that the Higher Education Proclamation encourages constructive competition, strategic partnership, mutual trust and collaboration between and among all providers of higher education. To this effect, the establishment of the Forum for Public Private Partnership (FPPP) is timely and crucial.

On top of these, the research team recommends an in-depth comparative study of the issues not treated by this study as well as on the contributions of both private and public HEIs to the overall development of the country. Such a study will provide policy makers and other stakeholders with more inputs to improve the situation and also provide a realistic assessment of the state of the higher education sector in the country.

## References

Addis Zemen News Letter, Hidar 28, 2004 E.C. Results and Decisions on the Performance Evaluation of Distance and Cross-border Education of Higher Education Institutions (Amharic Version). Addis Ababa.

AEPHEIs. 2009. Threatening the private higher education sector is diverting from the national agenda of educational quality. Addis Ababa, *Reporter Newsletter*, October 11, 2009.

Ashcroft K.2007. "Public private partnership in Ethiopian higher education: An analysis of the support the private sector needs to fulfill its potential contribution to the expansion of higher education". Proceedings of the fifth national conference on private higher education in Ethiopia. Addis Ababa: St. Mary's University College.

Bjarnason S. et al. 2009. *A new dynamic private higher education*. Paris: UNESCO.

Central Intelligence Authority (CIA). 2010. The world face book, USA.

Chang Da W. 2007. Public and private higher education institutions in Malaysia: Competing, complimentary or crossbreeds as education providers, *Kajiam Malaysia, Jld. XXV (1)*

Cheng K 2009. Public-private partnerships, in Bjarnason S. et. al. (2009). *A new dynamic private higher education*. Paris: UNESCO.

Damtew Teferra. 2005. Private higher education in Ethiopia : The current landscape. *International Higher Education*, 40. Retrieved on August 23, 2007,fromhttp://www.bc.edu/org/avp/soe/cihe/Newsletter/Number40/number40.htm

Daniel S. Alemu. 2010. Expansion Vs. quality: Emerging issues of for-profit private higher education institutions in Ethiopia. *International Review of Education*. 56 (1), 51-61.

Dill D. 2005. The public good, the public interest, and public higher education. PPAQ, University of North Carolina.

Duczmal D. 2006. *The rise of private higher education in Poland: Policies, markets and strategies.* CHEPS/UT. The Netherlands.

Ethio Channal Newsletter. 2010. Five private colleges fully closed, seven partially closed, 38 colleges given warning. 05(254), 20-21 (Amharic Version).

FDRE. 2009. Higher Education Proclamation (No. 650/2009). Addis Ababa : Birhanena Selam Printing Enterprise

Fielden J. and Varghese N.V. 2009. Regulatory issues, in Bjarnason S. et. al. 2009. *A new dynamic private higher education*. Paris: UNESCO.

Geiger Roger L. 1985. "The public and private sectors in higher education: A comparison of international patterns," *Higher Education*, 17(6): 699-711

Geiger R. L. 1986. Private sectors in higher education: Structure, function, and change in eight countries. In Duczmal, D. 2006. *The rise of private higher education in Poland: Policies, markets and strategies*. CHEPS/UT. The Netherlands.

Geiger, R. L. 1987. Private higher education. In P. G. Altbach (Ed.), International higher education: An encyclopedia, (Vol. 1). New York: Garland Publishing, Inc.

Gibbons, M. 1998. Higher education relevance in the 21st Century. Paper presented at The World Bank Human Development Week '98, Alexandria, Virginia, 4 - 6 March.

Gupta A. 2008. International trends and private higher education institutions in India. *International Journal of Education Management,* 22 (6).

Haileleul Zeleke. 2007. "Partnership between public and private higher education institutions in Ethiopia: Some key policy options". Proceedings of the fifth national conference on private higher education in Ethiopia. Addis Ababa: St. Mary's University College.

Hailemarkos A. 2006. "Need and satisfaction assessment of Ethiopian private higher education institutions on the broadcast media". Proceedings of the fourth national conference on private higher education institutions in Ethiopia. Addis Ababa: St. Mary's University College.

Harvey L. and Green D. 1993. Defining quality, *Assessment and Evaluation in Higher Education*, 18 (1).

HERQA. 2011. Results and Decision of the Performance Evaluation of Regular Programs of PHEIs. Addis Ababa: HERQA.

HERQA. 2009. Admas University College institutional quality audit report. Addis Ababa: HERQA.

HERQA. 2009. City University College institutional quality audit report. Addis Ababa: HERQA.

HERQA. 2009. Royal University College institutional quality audit report. Addis Ababa: HERQA.

HERQA. 2009. St. Mary's University College institutional quality audit report. Addis Ababa: HERQA.

HERQA. 2009. Unity University College institutional quality audit report. Addis Ababa: HERQA.

HERQA. 2008. List of pre-accredited and accredited institutions. Addis Ababa: National Printing Press PLC.

Johnstone D. B. 1998. The financing and management of higher education: A status report on worldwide reforms, the World Bank.

LaRocques N. 2008. Private higher education: Funding issues. Unpublished.

Levy D.C. 2007. "Private public interfaces in higher education development: two sectors in sync.?" In Gupta, A (2008). International trends and private higher education institutions in India. *International Journal of Education Management,* 22(6).

Levy D.C. 1980. Public policy and private higher education. *American Journal of Education,* 88 (2).

Marginson S. 2007. The Public/Private divide in higher education: A global revision. *Higher Education,* 53 (1).

Materu P. 2007. Higher education quality assurance in Sub-Saharan Africa: Status, challenges, opportunities, and promising practices. Washington, DC: The World Bank

Middleton C. 2000. Models of state and market in the 'Modernization' of higher education, *British Journal of Sociology of Education,* 21 (4): 537-55

Mikias Sebsibe. 2010. Education ministry bans distance learning. *Fortune Newsletter.* 11 (539), 1 & 8.

Ministry of Education. 2011. Education statistics annual abstract (2003 E.C./2010- 2011G.C.). Addis Ababa: EMIS, PRMD

MoFED. 2010. The Growth and transformation plan (GTP) of Ethiopia. Addis Ababa

Mok J.K & Lee M.H. 2001. Globalization and change of governance: Higher education reforms in Hong Kong, Taiwan and Mainland China. Unpublished.

Neave G. 2006. On incorporating the university, *Higher Education Policy,* 19(2).

Nganga G. 2010. Private universities to expand access. Retrieved on December 06, 2010, from http://www.universityworldnews.com

Nwuke K. 2008. The private provision of higher education in Ethiopia: Growth, challenges, and prospects. *JHEA/RESA*, 6 (1), 71–94.

OECD. 2006. Tertiary education for the knowledge society. Paris: OECD.

Pachuashvili M. 2009. The politics of higher education: Governmental policy choices and private higher education in post-communist countries. Dissertation (unpublished), Budapest

Reporter Newsletter. 2010. Forty two colleges/institutes operating in the SNNPR banned not to accept new entrants for the coming year. 15(44/1071), 3-4 (Amharic Version).

Reynolds P. A. 1990. 'Is an external examiner system an adequate guarantee of academic standards?', in Tam, M. 2001.Measuring Quality and Performance in Higher Education. *Quality in Higher Education, 7(1)*.

SMUC. 2008. Graduate tracer study: With a particular focus on graduates from the regular division (Unpublished).

Tam M. 2001. Measuring quality and performance in higher education. *Quality in Higher Education, Vol. 7(1)*.

Teixeira P. and Amaral A. 2001. Private higher education and diversity: An exploratory survey. *Higher Education Quarterly*, 55(4).

Thaver 2008. The private higher education sector in Africa: Current trends and themes in six country studies. *JHEA/RESA 6 (1), 127–142*

Tilak J.B.G. 1991. 'The privatization of higher education', Prospects, XXI(2), 227-239.

Varghese N.V. 2004. Patterns in ownership and operation of private higher education institutions. N. V. Varghese (ed.). *Private Higher Education*. Paris: IIEP/UNESCO.

Varghese N.V. 2006. Growth and expansion of private higher education in Africa. Paris: IIEP- UNESCO.

Vroeijenstijn T. 1992. "External quality assessment: Servant of two masters? The Netherlands university perspective". In Quality Assurance in Higher Education. Lewes: Falmer Press.

Wilkinson R. and Yussof I. 2005. Public and private provision of higher education in Malaysia: A comparative analysis. *Higher Education,* 50(3).

Wondwossen Tamirat. 2005. "Comparative Study of Country Laws on Private Higher Education: Possible Lessons for Ethiopia". Proceedings of the Third National Conference on Private Higher Education. Addis Ababa: St. Mary's University College.

Zha, Q. 2006. The resurgence and growth of private higher education in China. Ontario Institute for Studies in Education, University of Toronto

Zumeta, W. 1997. State policy and private higher education: Past, present and future. In J. Smart (ed), Higher Education: Handbook of Theory and Research. New York: Agathon Press.

# Notes about the Authors

**Wossenu Yimam** is an Assistant Professor with a PhD in Educational Administration. Besides his teaching career, he has served as Assistant Director of the Institute of Educational Research as well as Registrar of Addis Ababa University. He has also served as external quality auditor for HERQA, and team leader of nation-wide surveys and monitoring & evaluation activities conducted by international consulting firms. Dr. Wossenu has been actively engaged in series of research undertakings focusing on educational management in Ethiopia, on which he has published journal articles, book chapters and conference papers.

**Mulu Nega** has a PhD in higher education policy from the Center for Higher Education Policy Studies, University of Twente, the Netherlands. His dissertation is on 'Quality and Quality Assurance in Ethiopian higher Education: Critical Issues and Practical Implications'. He has authored a number of journal articles, book chapters and conference proceedings on quality issues in Ethiopian education. Moreover, he undertook a variety of consultancy services for governmental and nongovernmental organizations. Currently he is an assistant professor at the Institute of Educational Research, Addis Ababa University. In addition to his academic position, he has held various administrative positions such as Head of the Testing Center in Addis Ababa University, and Coordinator of donor-funded projects. He is now a Director of the Center for Academic Standards and Quality Enhancement, Addis Ababa University.

www.ingramcontent.com/pod-product-compliance
Lightning Source LLC
Chambersburg PA
CBHW021716230426
43668CB00008B/853